A Prophecy Twice Told

A PROPHECY TWICE TOLD

GLENN T. MOORE

To order additional copies of this book, contact:
Xlibris Corporation
1-888-795-4274
www.Xlibris.com
Orders@Xlibris.com
27952

CONTENTS

INTRODUCTION

A Prophecy Twice Told is a book written to help the student of the Bible with interpretation of the last prophetic books of the Bible, the Apocalypse or Revelation. It also helps those who are not totally familiar with the Bible to understand it, especially the Old Testament with its rich symbolic structure. For those who don't believe in the existence of God, it proves His existence through logic using the books of the Bible and the interplay of its characters and events. Excursions into characters and events of the Bible are also prevalent throughout the book, aiding clarity of the message, enabling growth of Bible students, and, hopefully, giving a vision that nonbelievers can grasp and gain and become believers. It can also help to deepen their faith in God.

The book is *not* an attempt to forecast or pinpoint the final end time since it is stated by Christ Himself that no one knows the exact time of the end except God the Father, but rather it's an attempt to prepare mankind for an emergent end of time and suggests that mankind, those who are wise, should be preparing themselves for this end. It is not a scare tactic because we all must end just as many before us have ended. Death is appointed to man. This we all must pass through. The book simply helps us to recognize the markers, the milestones that mark the end of this world by unraveling the last book of the Bible, the Apocalypse where the markers are found and strongly pronounced.

Many have been in awe of God, His power, His wisdom, and His love. The book is an attempt to help captivate its reader and propel him to the point where many others who have witnessed God, either profoundly or less profoundly. It also sets out to demonstrate that God actually exists and beckons all to Him as the prophets and many others have told. It is an attempt to satisfy the faithful, to quench their thirst for more of the Divine, and to kindle a faith for those who have none.

There is really no attempt to qualify the validity of the book. Its validity, since it is self-contained, as God is self-contained, qualifies it. It relies only on the logic that God imparted in the entire works of the Bible. The author, however, is a witness to God; and as a witness, He is attuned to him. I was told by God to write so that my witness may be made known and that those who have the wisdom to understand will understand and thus order their lives accordingly because once you vividly attune yourself to God, it would be foolish not to be saved, which was stated by the apostle Paul.

This book will help you to the point of realization that God exists. For those who have doubts, once that recognition is established, all doors to Him will be opened. The reader will gain insight into the Bible, its stories, and God will have a deeper meaning for him also. He will then allow God to take a more active role in his life. All of this will come into being because of the unraveling of the Apocalypse or Revelation (the two words will be used interchangeably in this text) and the analyzing of its symbolisms and terms.

CHAPTER 1

SYMBOLISM

Symbolism is an integral part of all of the prophetic books of the Bible. A lack of understanding of the symbolic role in these books will hamper a genuine study and appreciation of them. Symbolism is a necessary key.

In short, let a truth be stated. I say truth because just as everything else, the Bible contains complete and absolute logic. Why? God Himself is absolute; therefore, His very being is absolute. Meaning, He stands alone without the aid of any support. Everything is contained within Him or His consciousness. Nothing exits external of Him; hence, His word is absolute, needing no external support for proof. Since the Bible is the word of God, it is an absolute sense flowing on its own with self-supporting logic or reasoning.

Therefore, it is safe to state that the Bible is in perfect logic because it, as everything else, comes from God. Why is this? Because God made everything; therefore, all searches for explanation is to explain God or His creation. This is true for science, mathematics, astrology, etc. So whatever explanation that is obtained is also from God since He initially created it. Therefore, logic, the working of universal truths, is also from God because He created everything even the functioning of the mind and the self-contained order of reasoning. Man only comes along to explain God's works as He studies and gains knowledge of things, i.e., $E = mc^2$, formulated by Einstein. This formula gives us the inner makings of energy, which is present throughout the universe.

Since we understand that logic plays an important scheme in unraveling things and that God is the basis for logic, then we can proceed to unravel the Apocalypse using not man's learned logic about the function of order or reasoning but God's logic put into place so that man would understand the works of God, namely here, the prophecy of the Apocalypse, with that logic being absolute as all logic is absolute if the whole is proven. Of course, with God, all is absolute because He exists in an absolute state of being: omnipotent, omnipresent, and omniscient.

With all of this in mind, one can conclude that the logic of the Bible is absolute because God is absolute. A symbol can be a word, an object, or a thing. Second, all symbols remain consistent throughout the Bible, Old and New Testaments. Third, symbolism is simple and basic. Much of it comes from Old World knowledge but can be applied even in modern times. This is, of course, especially true for the Apocalypse, which takes place in both. Fourth, certain symbols are derived from actual occurrences in the Bible, i.e., sea of glass, derived from Noah's flood or the destruction of the world by water. Finally, nothing exists without being explained in some part or book of the Bible; most symbols are explained with the ones that are not being left to pure prophecy, by a person who is endowed by God to understand divine will, which can be directly given by God, spoken or relayed by Him through some divine means.

A Symbol as a Word, Object, or Thing

A symbol can be a word, an object, or a thing used vividly throughout the Bible. For example, in Daniel 5:5-25, the famous handwriting on the wall, spelled the end for Baltassar, king of Babylon. The words spelled out by the hand were "Mane: God hath numbered thy kingdom, and hath finished it. Thecel: Thou art weighed in the balance and art found wanting. Phares: Thy kingdom is divided and given to the Medes and Persians." These words were written as symbols of coming events on the wall in the king's palace and were interpreted by Daniel, endowed by God to understand His divine words. The meaning of these words are revealed by the prophet Daniel.

Another good symbol is the burning bush. The symbol of the bush first appeared in Genesis 22:13, where the ram, a replacement for Abraham's son Isaac as a sacrifice, was caught by the horns. The second time the bush was presented as a symbol was in Exodus 3:2. It was the fulfillment of the promise God had made to Abraham in Genesis 22:17. He had returned to free the Jewish nation and to make them a great nation by His miracles. The bush was merely a symbol of the promise and reminder that Abraham gave all to God and fervently obeyed him. Abraham was willing to give his only son Isaac as a sacrifice. God had promised Abraham Isaac in his old age. Abraham's willingness to sacrifice Isaac, his only son, proved that man was worthy of Christ whom God let suffer and die for our salvation. Christ was God's only begotten son.

The Consistency of the Symbolism

Any content using symbolism must have continuity as the system would be ineffective if this were not the case. This is especially true if the material covers different time spans, making it complex for that reason alone. It would be hard to trace meanings if the symbols changed meaning often, or at all. Since this is a given, man's understanding of the symbols must be constant when He communicates to other men. Think how much more so for God, who is flawless; therefore, His symbolism is flawless. He knows all of our limitations and makes allowances for them.

Of course, as mentioned earlier, God put everything on man's level so that man could grasp all that was intended for him. Therefore, the symbolism is constant in the Bible but with such greatness that it proves the greatness of God. Most of the books in the Bible were written at different times; yet the symbols remain flawless. For example, in Ezekiel 29:21, God tells the Jews that a horn will bud forth, and that He will give Israel an open mouth, meaning that in this captivity, Israel will have a leader. This leader refers to Daniel, who would be in Nabuchodonosor's and other kings of Babylon's houses as spokesmen, not only for Israel, but for the king also.

In Daniel 7:8, Daniel has a vision of four beasts. The fourth had ten horns, and as He noticed the horns, little horns sprang out of the midst of them. Three of the first horns were plucked out at this presence and behold, eyes like the eyes of a man were in one and a mouth speaking great things.

We can therefore trace the meaning of the symbol, horn, as a leader. It was explained in Ezekiel as such and when it reappears in Daniel, it has the same meaning—leader. The added details extend the meaning of leader by adding it had "eyes like the eyes of a man and a mouth speaking great things." This animated it for visual effects and a deeper understanding of it as a man who is a leader. The meaning of Daniel's vision will be interpreted later with more details because it plays a very important part in understanding the Apocalypse.

The Bible was written as it is in ancient days or time; therefore, the symbols are old-world symbols but are still the same and relevant in modern time. For example, in the Apocalypse, there are many passages where the symbols for a royal leader or head of state are depicted by the diadem or crown. The symbol is very basic or understood by all. But since we are in modern times and monarchy is not a common thing or different forms of governments have evolved, then we can see that the symbolic meaning is not in the literal sense. A diadem should not be construed as a king per se but could mean a leader as a head of state since a position as a king in biblical days was also a head of state or kingdom.

Understandably so, God placed these symbols in a manner where both old-world man and modern man could grasp the intended meaning of them. Only God knows the end of time for man and with that thought, many years can elapse with many changes. (The Apocalypse was written many years ago, and many have tried to guess the end; yet the world still exists in the same state as it was during the time the Apocalypse was revealed to St. John.) Therefore, the symbolic system or structure of the Bible allows time to lapse by not limiting its symbols to specific epochs or eras, but rather they can be understood in a broader sense or meaning at any time.

The Symbolism Is Basic and Simple

Most symbols in the Bible are not only basic, but they are also simple. Understandably, this allows all level of understanding. The way the symbols are used leaves less chance for error or misinterpretations. If we understand that God is a loving God, who wants all of us with him, then we can see that this is why the Bible is not complex, because this would cause many not to understand the Bible, especially the poor man whose limited exposure to things is sometimes a stumbling block for him. Therefore, in His infinite wisdom, God has left His written word in a simple and basic form for all mankind to grasp, regardless of his stature in life because He has love for us all, especially the poor and downtrodden. It was evident in Christ's ministry; it was manifested in the beatitudes.

Certain Symbols Are Taken from Occurrences in the Bible

Many of the symbols used are taken from occurrences in the Bible. The sea of glass was used as a symbol. It occurred in the book of Genesis. It is symbolic of the destruction of the world by water. Two major symbols were taken from this event and are mentioned throughout the Bible, especially Revelation. They are the sea of glass at the foot of the throne and the emerald rainbow above the throne. Of course, we know that God destroyed the race of man, except for Noah and his seed, with water and afterward, as a symbol that the world would never be destroyed again by water, God placed a rainbow in the heavens. These two are prominent but there are many other occurrences used as symbols in the Bible. Also, these two are used throughout the Apocalypse because they were physical occurrences used in the first destruction and are meant as symbols suggesting another end of things in the Apocalypse.

Most Symbolisms Are Explained in Some Books of the Bible

Most symbolism in the Bible are explained in some part or book of the Bible. This is done because the books are not only a historical recording of God's intervention with man, but they are also instruments of instruction for man, or God's will for man. Since the latter is true, even if it is in the negative sense of punishment for sins, there are no obscurities contained in it because the lessons have to be clear in order for limited man to understand how He should be to be a true son of God. So why obscure it with no chance of man unraveling it? Jesus taught in parables to capture His audience, but yet unraveled many for them to understand. This is also true with God.

Most of the early books contained many prophecies, which were given by God with symbolism, then fulfilled. This in itself is a lesson on how to interpret the symbolism since all of it is constant and will never change in meaning, no matter where it is found in the Bible: Old or New Testament. In Ezekiel 17, God gives a prophecy in a parable. It was the prophecy of two eagles and a vine.

First, God told the parable on how two eagles both took the marrow of the cedar and planted it elsewhere and it became a mighty vine. Later, He explained one eagle as Nabuchodonosor, the king of Babylon and the second eagle as Himself. Nabuchodonosor would capture Israel and nurse it back to health because of Daniel's service to God.

The second eagle, God Himself, delivers the Jews from captivity, and by bringing Christ from Abraham's seed, Christ, the Messiah, leads mankind to God. Thus, the prophecy is told, explained, and completed. In this example, one-half of the prophecy is accomplished in the beginning of the book of Daniel, the captivity of the Jewish nation by Nabuchodonosor; the other half is accomplished with the birth of Jesus.

As evident by the foregoing examples, many symbols maintain the characteristics of that physical symbol. For example, an eagle, whose nature or characteristic is keen eyes, vision because he spots his food at great heights and dives for it then carries it off. This is especially true if it is stated that the eagle is flying, peering for food. A bear has great strength; a lion, ferocity. These are all examples of physical things, creatures used to demonstrate, symbolically, a human possessing like qualities. And as stated, these symbols do not change and are constant throughout the Bible, Old and New Testaments.

Divine qualities are also heightened by the nature of the symbols. The eagle has keen eyes as its nature but the equation to divine quality is keen insight into God. St. John the Evangelist is often called an eagle because of his great insight into God, which is denoted in his Gospel. We can further see the eagle as such by the salvation of Nabuchodonosor who was saved by God Himself. God brought Nabuchodonosor to a very lowly, inhumane state in Daniel 4:30

in order to save him because Nabuchodonosor was an instrument of God. God gave him all the might that He possessed, and for him to claim all the credit as his own was blasphemous to God. However, his encounter with God gave Nabuchodonosor a deep profound insight into God. He could see and actually feel the greatness of God, which attuned him to God in Daniel 4:31 and 32, as others who were touched by him, for example St. Paul. Through that chastisement, Nabuchodonosor was saved.

Symbols in the Bible are very important to understand its prophetic books, which are rich with symbolism. That these symbols remain constant throughout the Bible regardless of the book it is used in, show that God placed these symbols in a manner where man could grasp them and build on them. He left many to prophecy, and they can only be unraveled by a prophet whom God has endowed with divine reasoning. But yet many are left for the way Christ terms it, "those who have wisdom, let him understand." With that we can proceed to the Apocalypse and unravel its meaning.

CHAPTER 2

GOD'S APPEARANCE TO ST, JOHN

St. John was captive on an island named Patmos when God came to him in a vision in Revelation 1:12-16. "And I turned to see the voice that was speaking to me. And having turned, I saw seven golden lamp-stands; and in the midst of the seven lamp-stands one like to a son of man, clothed with a white garment reaching to the ankles, and girt about the breast with a golden girdle. But his head and his hair were white as white wool, and as snow and his eyes were as a flame of fire; his feet were like fine brass, as in a glowing furnace, and his voice like the voice of many waters. And he had in his right hand seven stars. And out of his mouth came forth a sharp two edged sword; and his countenance was like the sun shinning in its power."

In this passage, God the father Himself appears to St. John. God the Father in symbolism is always separated from Christ by having white hair and a white beard, His actual physical appearance. The white hair is a symbol of age and wisdom; God always was and always will be. Christ is symbolized by being the lamb that shed His blood for man's salvation. Also, He gave it to St. John by saying He is "the Alpha and the Omega," which are always the words of God the Father.

As living proof that He was the living God, He appeared with seven golden lamp stands signifying God's seven churches. It was also a reference as to when

God instructed the building of the tabernacle. He told Moses in Numbers 8:1-4, "And the Lord spoke to Moses, saying: speak to Aaron, and thou shalt say to him: When thou shalt place the seven lamps, the candlestick be set up on the south side. Give orders therefore that the lamps look over against the north, towards the table of the loaves of proposition, over against that part shall they give light toward which the candlestick looketh. And Aaron did so, and he put the lamps upon the candlestick, as the Lord had commanded Moses. Now this was the work of the candlestick, it was of beaten gold, both the shaft in the middle, and all that came out of both sides of the branches: according to the pattern which the Lord had shown to Moses, so he made the candlestick."

This is the same candlestick that God held in His hand, thus proving He was God the Father through that symbolic gesture. He was the same god who ordered Moses to make the same golden lamp stands. Know that these symbolic gestures are not only for the person viewing them but also for the audiences who will hear about the events in the years to come until the end of time.

The symbolism continues with God being girded about the breast with a golden girdle, symbolizing a warrior. As God is prepared to war with Satan and his evil forces, the symbolism infers that the final war with Satan will take place and God will effect an end to his temptation of man for a while. We will later see that Satan will be loose again to tempt man, as a final test of salvation.

Throughout time, God has fought for man. In each book of the Bible, there is always evidence where God has overthrown the devil for man. For example, in Daniel's time, God saved Sidrach, Misach, and Abdenago from the fiery furnace in Daniel 3:46-50. These men stated staunchly that they would not adore any god but the God of their fathers, even if it meant their death.

The vision of God being girded is the same God who is ready to save mankind if mankind would heed His words and keep His commandments. He is ready to wage war for them always.

The symbolism that says "eyes were as a flame of fire; his feet were like fine brass, as in a glowing furnace," has to do with purification of sin. In Malachias 3:2 and 3, God states that Christ is "like a refining fire, refining and cleansing metal and purifying the sons of Levi." The cleansing of metal is equated to the cleansing of souls. Therefore, God's eyes see all and the evil that He sees will be cleansed.

The brass feet glowing like a furnace symbolizes the wine press of wrath in Apocalypse 14:10. In the olden days, grapes were pressed by foot to produce wine. Here the symbolism is complete from the awareness of the sins of man to God's wrath of punishment for sin.

St. John says that God's voice was the voice of many waters, which symbolizes total destruction as in the case of the great flood that destroyed the whole of mankind. God symbolizes by His voice that once again the earth will be destroyed and made anew and that man's imperfect system will come to an end.

The seven stars in His right hand are the seven angels of the seven churches, and the seven lamp stands are the seven churches.

In symbolic form is the two-edged sword that comes out of the mouth of God. This symbolizes death to those who have not kept God's commandments. As we will see in the next paragraph, this symbolism later in the scripture will also be used when this is passed from Father to Jesus.

Many times throughout His ministry, Jesus explained that He and the Father are one. In the last paragraph, St. John explains that when he saw Jesus, he fell at Jesus's feet, "as one dead." And Jesus told him not to be afraid, that He is "the First and the Last, and He who lives, I was dead, and behold, I am living forevermore; and I have the key of death and of hell." This statement tells St. John He is Christ who has overcome death.

Through dialogue, we can see that both God the Father and Christ have appeared to St. John. God the Father's dialogue at the beginning states that He is "the Alpha and the Omega," which He always uses plus the visual image of white hair and beard. Christ at the end, through His dialogue, mentioned being "the First and the Last," which He used during His ministry and for the fact that He conquered death. Therefore, it is vividly expressed as Christ had said that He and the Father are one and that at the end He, Christ, would come again to claim His church and those who have lived the law (Rom 2:15-16). The church being the devoted followers of Christ, who came to us as the word of God made flesh, and the others before Him who followed the law and the law that was written on the hearts of others.

The distinction of the deity, God the Father and Christ, is always expressed. At first, it is not discernible; but if a close inspection and perusal is done, it is easily discerned that the two deities are expressed and separated using euphemisms such as the alpha and omega for God the Father and the first and the last for Christ. The two mean the same, but each uses only one in particular constantly throughout the Bible.

Christ died at the age of thirty-three in the prime of His life, not aged. Therefore, He would not appear in a manner that is foreign and not consistent. Remember, symbolist structure cannot change, or it would be too difficult to follow. Therefore, the white-headed being is God the Father, the white hair being an indication of age and wisdom.

There is not a description of God the Father recorded; the patriots of old gave no description of Him. It could be that He never showed Himself to them or it could be it was never recorded. However, the fact remains that the two separate beings are depicted in the appearance to St. John.

We know through biblical writings that God exist in a tristate: the Father, the Son, and the Holy Spirit, which is known as the Trinity. It is not understood by mankind how this is achieved, three beings in one, but is accepted through faith as a reality.

Many times Christ said that He and the Father are one; and if you saw one, you've seen the other (Jn 10:30, 14; Jn 14:6). He did not differentiate that He meant appearance or substance, but the latter would be appropriate since Christ prayed constantly to the Father. Although implied that Christ was in the same substance as the Father, He always spoke in subordination to the Father, which meant His substance, although the same, was lesser in power. Thus, we have two distinct beings, but they are of the same substance.

God does exist. In Genesis, it is written that God created man in His image and likeness. The proof of His existence is in the fact that God and man exist in a tristate. God is in three: the Father, the Son, and the Holy Spirit. Man is in three: the conscience, ego, and superego. Sigmund Freud unraveled the mind for us, and through hypnosis the three are revealed or reached.

God's three persons possess all powers of His conscious state and are separated from each other but still are one, just as man's are. Each of God's beings functions on His own level, is aware of the other, and can converse with the other because of their supreme nature.

God's existence is obvious. He states through His written word that He created man in His image and likeness. In His image and likeness, He created man. God and man exist in a tristate. The logic is completed, a manifested likeness.

Perhaps mankind has difficulty understanding God's powers but only knows that His powers exist. Finite vision has much to do with man's ability to understand God . . . completely. I only gave it to you as a proof of God's existence as I said this book would. There are many that will be given!

CHAPTER 3

LETTERS TO THE CHURCHES

In chapters 2 and 3, God tells St. John what to write to each of the seven churches. Each letter to the individual churches, which numbered seven, promises eternal salvation for the worthy and damnation to those who didn't heed God's words. We know that this is God the Father talking because in chapter 4, He speaks again. "After this, after the writing to the seven churches, I looked, and behold, a door standing open in heaven, and the former voice, the voice heard in the opening vision which was God the Father which I had heard as of a trumpet speaking with me, said, 'Come up hither.'" The voice was the same; therefore, it was God the Father's voice, not Christ.

God speaks to righteous men only and only a very few men in the history of earth have been righteous enough for God to speak to. The first time God spoke to St. John, He disguised His voice in the tone of many waters, which symbolizes that the first destruction of earth was done by water, flooding. The symbolism is that He has come to instruct St. John for his mission of prophecy on the second destruction of earth or His system installment and to eradicate man's imperfect system.

Note that everything is in symbolism, the real reason why God did not use His true voice with St. John, who was a very righteous man. The symbolism used must equate events, which validate the appearance to the upcoming generations. These events happened many years prior to St. John's revelation but are consistent with the message that God sends to mankind.

At the time of St. John's prophecy, the church was in its infancy stages, or rather Christ had sent the Holy Spirit, and the apostles were on their mission. The writing to the seven churches could have a dual meaning just as the meaning of the ten-horned beast—it is superimposed. The first meaning, the actual seven churches mentioned, and the second, the actual churches at the end of the world as we know it now.

It would be most logical for the second condition to prevail here since Revelation is written for modern times. It takes place in a time different from St. John's era, at least the last stages are in a time frame that is not of St. John's, that being the end. Therefore, the warning is for the end, although the impact, in a Christian sense, should be felt at either end of the time frame because God's warning to His churches to be holy and dutiful is a constant thing. The emphases is placed on the end because this is the reason for the prophecy—to warn that there will be an ending in the manner revealed to St. John.

Also, if we note that throughout the reading of letters to the churches, the words "I will come upon thee as a thief and thou shalt not know at what hour I shall come upon thee," and others words to that effect are indications that the message is time consumed; but since these words appear at the very end of Revelation, then we can see the meaning is mainly meant for the end.

Since the meaning or impact is mainly meant for the end, we can see that many years have elapsed since St. John's time, with many changes. Just who are the seven churches, if they apply to today's situation?

Before this can be answered, the mind must be cleared of cluttered human thinking. God must be envisioned as He really is, not as what one wants Him to be because it fit the purpose. If God is all, than how can we apply it to this situation?

If God is all, and He is, then He must have a complete understanding of man's character and nature that is terribly flawed. Therefore, God knew that we would somehow or another branch off into other religions because of differences, which is the nature of man. This was evident even with the apostles who were with Christ. Many times Christ had to settle arguments on who was the greatest apostle and who took the more important role, to which Christ stated, "The last will be first, and the first last" (Mt 20:16). Also, while the apostles where out on a mission, they came across someone else doing the same thing they were doing: healing, casting out demons, and the like, and they stopped them. When they returned, they told Christ about what they had seen and done. Christ answered, "Those who are for you are not against you. Do not stop them."

It could be possible that the foregoing was allowed to instill even at that time before the apostles received the Holy Spirit, that there would be other churches walking the same road since their mission at that time was a trial run before their actual mission, to see how they would do. Christ sent them out as novices to teach them or instruct them on their upcoming mission and to give them the confidence that they would need to succeed. Christ, as part of the Trinity knowing what they would encounter, further enlightened them realizing that many others would learn of the many events once recorded. Think of it as God telling His own that there will be many others spreading the word, others also chosen by God to do so. The statement alludes to some workings that God has put into place that is apart from them, yet accomplishing the same thing.

Therefore, we can see that God in His infinite wisdom made allowances for man, maybe not just the apostles but men who came after them. This is not to say that God is subject to man in any way because He is not, rather, He suffers men in abilities knowing that man is flawed and helpless. At the same time, however, God placed the Holy Spirit over His church knowing that nothing can be done without His aid, and the Holy Spirit accomplishes all. He, the Holy Spirit, is honored by the Father Himself, hinting that the Holy Spirit is supreme in the other two eyes—esteemed.

It is written that insults are suffered by the Father and Christ and forgiven; not the case with the Holy Spirit. Therefore, the church is incapable of perishing in such capable hands, no matter what the human element does as ministers of the church and that if it is done in the name of God, it is done for His church. God in this sense means the Trinity. There have been many errors and hateful things done by ministers, but the Church still stands today as a beacon of salvation for all.

Not thinking in our human limited sense, how far reaching is the word of God, or to how many was the word in trusted? Let's ponder on this as stated without our human misgivings.

First, his legal son gave the word of God to the Jews, who were the direct descendants of Abraham. Secondly, Abraham had another son, who was not by his wife but whom God said He would bless because he too was Abraham's seed. And third, Christ came through Abraham's legal lineage stating that He had come not to change the law of the prophets but rather to fulfill them (Mt 5:17-18). Christ included the gentiles as children of God also, not just Jews and Arabs (Rom 15:12).

The Jewish nation is a story with which we are all familiar since Christ was born within the race of these chosen people. Christ came to save the world. He was Jewish.

The story of Ishmael is a different story; it is a story that was a brief moment in the life of Abraham, yet a very important one. Why? Because of the promise of God to make his people great. "Abraham, your seed shall be great!" (Gn 21:18) How much weight does your promise carry? How much more so for God? Also, Ishmael had twelve sons through which a nation was born; this symbolized that God the Father had worked that miracle. The other generation, springing from twelve sons was Abraham's legal son Isaac; but before the twelve sons were born, three generations had to pass to honor the Trinity. The three generations were Abraham, Isaac, and Jacob. Jacob of course had twelve sons who became the twelve tribes of Israel. Therefore, we can see that Ishmael plays an important role with God. The symbolism is there also with his having twelve sons that went on to become a mighty nation.

Most Christians do not know much about the Islamic religion, the religion of the Arabs, Ishmael's descendants. The only thing that we do know is that an angel of the Lord instructed or gave laws to Mohammed, the Islamic prophet, and this is how the religion was formed or began. They, as the Jews, do not believe in Jesus Christ as being God. Christ is held in esteem as being a major prophet. But there is a direct correlation between the Jews and Arabs, Muslims as the followers of Mohammed are called. Ishmael was helped by an angel, and it was stated that God was with Ishmael (Gn 21:20). God was also with the Jewish nation, which makes it a direct correlation but one that is not mentioned or hardly mentioned.

We can see from that example how great God's love for Abraham was. Ishmael, whom Abraham was told to cast out of his camp because of the feud between Sara, Abraham's wife and Isaac's mother, and Hagar, Sara's handmaid and Ishmael's mother (Gn 21:9-14). This Abraham did reluctantly because he loved Ishmael dearly also, yet Ishmael and his mother were cast out. But God was with Ishmael and blessed him even though he was not a direct heir to Abraham. God even sent an angel to save Ishmael's life (Gn 21:15-20).

There will be an attempt to correlate the will of God through the Jewish nation to the Arab nations, whom an angel tended, with the intent to show that God also provided for Ishmael and that he was not left out of God's love or His promise of greatness. However, the mainstay of God is Christianity, with Christ, because He is the promised one of God, but He is also integral with the Jews who deny Him as a person of God as do the Arabs or Islamic faith.

Islam as a religion had its beginning with a prophet known as Mohammed, who was given a revelation. This revelation stated specifically how God wanted the Arab nations to be in terms of behavior to Him, the Lord, Allah. It was also a rule of order for their behavior to man himself. It stressed punishment for those who did not obey God's law and reward for those who did. The reward given would be paradise. The punishment, of course, would be hell. This revelation was written in a book called the Holy Quran and was conveyed by an angel through the senses of Mohammed.

Before Mohammed, there were other prophets who brought words from God. But until Mohammed, the Arabs were a fragmented nation worshipping idols with no concept of God. These Muslim prophets Hud and Salih were between Noah and Abraham's time with another prophet Shu'aib placed after Abraham (*Major Theme of the Qur'an*, Fazlur Rahman). The Jewish prophets are all mentioned in the religion—those being Noah, Abraham, and Moses—and of course Jesus was placed as a prophet and not a person of the Trinity.

Mohammed brought unity to the Arab nations, a unity that helped to bond them and make them prosper. Today, the Arab nations are wealthy nations just as the Jewish nation. The deserts that they camped on as nomads, thus gaining rights to, are saturated with oil. Therefore, it is obvious that God's promise to make Abraham's seed great was kept, for the wealth of the Arabs have helped them to flourish just as the wealth of the Jews have help them to flourish in the world. They both are mighty nations with vast populations of people as God promised. Their wealth will sustain them and foster their further development if they abide by the laws that God has set for them—the same laws that Christ came to expound on and teach the ways of the elders so that upon His death the previous generations and the generations to follow could be saved.

Paradise is again open now, opened by the death of Christ, the sacrifice. God kept His word that was made from the beginning to Adam, that of His sending His only begotten Son to open the gates of heaven again for those who want it, although in an ambiguous manner but later explained by angels. It was stated thusly: "I will put enmities between thee and the woman, and thy seed and her seed; she shall crush thy head and thou shall lie in wait for her heel" (Gn 3:15). The Judean or Hebrew text reads, "Thou shall strike at her heel and she will strike at thy head," indicating the strife between good and evil. The foregoing passage illuminates the end where Satan is defeated.

The woman of course is the Virgin Mary, Christ's mother. By giving birth to Christ, she fulfilled the promise of God to send a savior to the world. It was obscured. However, God meant it to be so because as time would pass, mankind would be able to see that this has actually happened. The writings are too far apart in terms of years, yet they complement each other, proving the existence of God. The writing begins in Genesis 3:15 and again in Isaiah 7:14. Christ was born some 650 years after Isaiah.) Inference to Christ exists throughout the writings until the angel appears to Mary announcing the birth of Christ (Mt 1:18-25, Lk 1:26-38) many years after the event in the garden, but all the faithful waited for the Messiah.

We can see the vast power of God as even His promise is evident to this day—the promise to Abraham. There is no mistake that the seed of Abraham is great: Jacob and the Jewish nation and Ishmael and the Arab nations. But this should not take away from the initial promise of the Messiah who came through the Jewish nation.

To regress a bit, although Jesus was placed as a prophet, it is mentioned in the Holy Quran that Jesus was born through a miracle of God, per se, that the Holy Spirit conceived Christ, which is in keeping with the Christian teaching. But the idea of the Trinity is not believed or taught by Islam. It is believed that although Christ was of a miraculous birth, He was not God because the Holy Spirit was not considered to be God but only an angel or spirit who God sends to do His will. Therefore, Jesus as God is claimed by Islam to be an error in Christianity because of this misconception, thereby negating the existence of the Trinity.

Skeptics say that Islam was born out of the association of the Arab nations with both Judaism and Christianity in Mecca, where Mohammed lived. The religion itself is basically the same as Judaism and Christianity, the belief in one God with devotion to Him. Also expected of believers are good deeds, actions, and intentions towards one's fellow man. If those conditions do not prevail, then God condemns the soul to hell. The parallel is held as an association, but the religion is too well laid to be contrived by man, or if contrived by man, it had to be willed by God for man's sake because the avenues to God are there.

There are many things that suggest that Islam was sent to the Arabs as an avenue to God. First, God promised Abraham that Ishmael would become a great nation. If no other sign is visible, then the wealth of the Arabs is clearly visible. The wealth of their nation is the same as the Jewish nation. That wealth has enabled both to flourish in the world. Secondly, since God's promise was a complete promise, not just material because God is not material, it is evident that God also provided provision for their spiritual wealth through the Islamic religion, which was very fragmented until Mohammed's revelation. Remember that Ishmael was not the legal heir of Abraham; therefore, God, Himself told Abraham to heed Sara's wishes to put Ishmael out of their house. Hence, the dramatics are not there as with the Jews, mighty miracles and the like, but the love of Abraham by God is.

Christ was also a promise as was the promise to Abraham that his seed would be great. But Christ was a promise to the world as a savior. Although neither the

Jews nor the Arabs recognize Christ as the Messiah, Islam does. Christianity encompasses the world as is stated in the Bible. Christ came and brought eternal salvation through His ministry and, of course, His sin offering of death on the cross. The sin offering was for all mankind; therefore, Christ is the total or absolute promise, He is for everyone.

There are many things taught about Jesus, but one clear thing that He made specific was that He came to fulfill the law of the prophets, not to change one word (Mt 5:17). He also emphasized that every word of the prophets would come to pass with their words standing for all time until all things have been accomplished (Mt 5:18). Therefore, we can see that Christ, although being God and a person of the Trinity, based His ministry on the Old Law; but His ministry would know no boundaries and that ministry would be preached to every nation of the world before the end.

Just by Christ's statement, "I came to fulfill the Law," suggests that He had come to complete the law of the prophets in its fullest sense. Only Christ as God could do this because He has the power, which was given by the Father for Him to do so. Since He was God in the flesh, many things were satisfied or made clear by Him before He was slain for our sins. Among those things are the laws about marriage; another is stoning for sin (Mt 19:9, Jn 8:1-11). These two examples also show where the Mosaic Laws had gone astray. Of course, Christ as God has infinite love for man, and this was displayed constantly when He was with us. It is this love that leads man to God. "I am the light, the truth, and the way"; no man can see God but through me; follow my teachings and gain eternal life. This is my commandment, that you love one another as I have loved you" (Jn 15:12).

The above passage illustrates how imperfect humankind is. Christ had to put straight the law on marriage. "It was not so in the beginning to leave your wife for another, but rather cling to one wife for life, save for immorality" (Mt 19:9). He stated that Moses was pressed hard about the subject of divorce and complied. Stoning for sin was another law set straight. "He who is without sin cast the first stone" (Jn 8:7).

It is easy for mankind to stray from the Divine because mankind has his own ends, his own agendas. Also, without the divine, humankind is limited to his own flawed mental processes. God gave the Holy Spirit to the churches to help guide them. This is not meant to hinder the making of new laws because things do change and new laws are often times needed written, but care must be taken because of the holiness of God and His purpose.

As a result, we understand that God made two promises. One, the promise of His only son Christ, and two, an individual promise to a man, Abraham, who would willingly sacrifice His only son to God without question or hesitation, just on faith. Both promises were completed to the extent of perfection that only God can achieve, and both promises were made for the love of mankind.

The churches that are mentioned in Revelation are all the Christian churches of the world: the Catholic Church as well as the Protestant, in which there are twelve denominations (*The Religions of Man*, Huston Smith, Harper, and Row 1965, p. 347). They have branched off as Christ suggested to the apostles when He told them not to stop anyone from doing what they, the apostles, were doing. There will be no attempt to identify these churches, but if the history of the church is known, then the church can be identified. Regardless of the identity, the message is still the same: to be holy and dutiful for "I, Christ, will come quickly, and no one knows the day, the hour, or the second except the Father" (Mt. 24:42 and Mk. 13:35).

CHAPTER 4

THE THRONE OF GOD

In chapter 4, St. John tells how he went into the spirit and went into heaven. He reports, "There was a throne set in heaven, and upon the throne, one was sitting. And He who sat was in the appearance like to a jasper stone and a Sardis, and there was rainbow round about the throne, in the appearance like to an emerald."

God ended the world once with water and promised never to end the world again by the same means, which is symbolized by the emerald rainbow. Green symbolizes death, suggesting the world was too imperfect or green, which was the reason for His destroying it rather than man destroying it as we will find out later. Knowledge is the thing that makes it green. Yes, the world is very young in knowledge and prone to imperfection. Knowledge has to be accumulated through trial and error; then, documented as a true fact. This is to include all ramifications, science, nature, agriculture, society, etc. It has to be learned and proven by time.

God did not intend for the world to be subject to knowledge but rather tended by the Holy Spirit in His extreme perfection. Man would live in a paradise tended by the Holy Spirit. This means that he didn't have to worry about agricultural blights, diseases, etc., because the Holy Spirit would keep things perfect for man.

If Adam had not sinned, we would be the same in terms of learning, but learning in a state of innocence. With the aid of the Holy Spirit, man would have experienced things and recorded them, but would not have been subjected to them. This is to include habits that form the brunt of mass problems. Everything is habit forming to man: cigarettes, drugs, coffee, etc. The habitualness of almost everything destroys man.

A hypothetical example of how learning would have occurred if Adam had not sinned is this: every person who lives in a mountainous terrain knows not to walk on fallen trees or logs in the forest to cross them because there is a great danger of injuring oneself by falling. The logs are always moist, especially those that still have their bark on them. The moisture lay underneath the bark and cause slipping when stepped or walked on.

In Adam's true world, he would have walked on a log and slipped but would not have fallen. The Holy Spirit would have righted him before he would have hit the ground. This is true for all dangerous occurrences, with no harm being done to man's person.

However, through that experience, Adam would have retained the knowledge not to step on fallen trees. It is a hypothetical example, but should get across the world that we missed through sin. The perils would have been there, but there would have been no effect or injury from them.

This is why the term green is used and denoted for death. In our knowledge, we die. God's mind is not our mind. When we think, we think in one dimension: the real, what was defined for us by God. When God thinks, His mind encompasses the past, present, and future in a moment because He has those elements at His command. When the symbol was thought of, He knew that the color green would be used as a term to denote novelty.

Other important symbols—jasper and sardius stone—tell the story in themselves about the war with Satan over the inhabitants of earth. The sardius stone is the first stone used in Exodus 28:17. The sardius stone, or rather the precious stones, twelve in total, records the names of the children of Israel, Jacob's twelve sons, with the jasper being the sixth and also a green stone. The number 6 is an imperfect number and is the reason God destroyed earth or brought to end its system, man's system. The number 6 marks the number of the day that God created man. Now, man is with his knowledge, which he choose of his own free will and is extremely imperfect. The things that are innate to the Holy Spirit have to be learned by man, and man cannot master or attain the complete knowledge needed to sustain things. His reasoning results in so much waste and destruction.

Later in Revelation, God assigns the number 666 to man's system. In the Trinity, 3 means it is in extreme perfection. By numeration of 6 three times means that it is in extreme imperfection, which earth is, in comparison to God.

The earth had become too wicked and too imperfect. Now one can see why jasper (green) is used for the sixth stone. The world is too inexperienced in all facets to sustain itself, and when the world gets too wicked because of lack of instruction to a large extent, God chastises its wickedness. It doesn't have the knowledge or talent to survive. Knowledge will always give way to God because He is knowledge.

An example of how God's knowledge is in conjunction with man is the fact that God give us things that are complete. A miracle cure produces the end result. When man attempts to cure, he has to try many different things to effect that cure. In the case of penicillin, which is bread mold, it attacks microscopic cells called germs and kills them. It is the germs that cause many diseases. God only has to will that the diseases leave and it is gone. Man has to find the right ingredient to run the culprit gene away. As with the case of cancer, the process can take many years. Knowledge has to be gained before the situation is remedied. This is the case for all of man's distresses.

To throw out food for thought. In the foregoing passage, it was stated that penicillin was derived from bread mold. It is a cure for many dreaded diseases, a miracle drug it was defined when it first was discovered. It was life giving. Throughout the Bible, we note that Christ is the bread of life. Is there a connection with the two? Did God allow bread mold to give life as a sign that His son Christ is the bread of life and remind mankind who is in control? Remember who created everything!

The third stone is emerald, the same color of the rainbow that is around the throne. The emerald rainbow symbolizes the Trinity, God in three persons; the third stone is emerald, symbolizing the two; three, representing the three distinct persons in the Trinity. It was the Trinity's decision to destroy the world and, after its destruction, to make the promise not to destroy it again. Therefore, one can see the unity of the Trinity: God the Father on the throne is green and the Trinity is green, which is denoted by the third stone's being emerald.

Note also that God will begin to avenge the martyrs following the fourth seal, which is green, a pale green, however. The actual verbiage about the martyrs being avenged is found in the fifth seal. Further, the sardius stone is a clear stone, or blemish free, flawless. Later in subsequent chapters, when God completes the destruction of earth, the places of the stones will be turned around with the jasper first and the sardius sixth. This indicates that the imperfections are removed; God's system, or Christ, will reign.

Around the throne, St. John noted four living creatures full of eyes before and behind. The four living creatures play an important part in the sequence of events that begins Revelation. St. John continued to describe them. "And the first living creature is like a lion; and the second, like a calf, and the third has the face, as if were, of a man; and the fourth is like an eagle flying. And the four living creatures have each of them six wings; round about and within, they are full of eyes."

The four living creatures that St. John sees are the first four seals. The four living creatures symbolize the seals. These four living creatures are cherubim who depict men who have lived on earth, with one still living. The first, if put in conjunction with the first seal, represents England and her kings, beginning with Richard Plantagenet, or Richard the Lionheart. This is why the first creature is symbolized as a lion. The second is like a calf. This calf symbolizes idolatry or worshiping of gods or no belief in God. The symbol was taken from Genesis. It is the same golden calf that the Jews made while Moses was on the Mount Sinai.

Japan was pagan before World War II and still largely is pagan with Buddhism and Hinduism the main religions. If these are placed with the second seal, their meaning become clear as the slaughter or the loss of life. World War II was a war in which many lives were lost, and peace was taken from the earth.

The third creature was like that of a man. Here, again, placed with the third seal, the symbolism becomes clear. In this time frame or time period, there was much injustice done to man. The leadership of one man freed a race of men or races of men. Dr. Martin Luther King Jr. was the man who freed many minority races. He brought justice to the world, which is symbolized by the balanced scale told in the third seal.

The fourth is like and eagle, the great bald eagle, the bird of the United States of America. This person is endowed with great insight into God and the Divine Will. This seal symbolizes the end of the first sequence, or the beginning of the end. As the fourth seal ends, the martyrs are told to rest a little longer, signifying that the period of time remaining is short. The time for the Second Coming of Christ no one knows. Only God the Father knows the time of the end. Jesus Himself does not know the time of the end. (Each seal will be discussed entirely as they appear in sequence.)

The symbolism of the four living creatures here is similar to the symbolism to the four evangelists in Ezekiel who were represented by the cherubim (Ez 1:5-10). In Ezekiel, however, they all had four wings representing their mission for Christ. Christ's lineage was the fourth tribe of Israel, Juda "the Lion." They all had for the soles of their feet, calf's feet sparking like glowing brass, meaning the ending of ungodliness, such as idolatry and sinfulness. This was their mission and their gospels are preached throughout the world. The glowing furnace presented earlier means the end of imperfections. Their faces were the faces of men, meaning godly. The face of a lion on the right side of all the four means their gospel is forceful. The face of an ox on the left of all the four means they were dutiful, and the face of an eagle over all the four means they were divine and keen in the word of God.

The cherubim, therefore, gives the characteristics of the men they represent, and they animated by symbolism the person who will perform the mission. In Ezekiel it was the four evangelists; in Revelation they represented the four men who sat upon the horses. Also, the cherubim function as the angel who will help complete the mission, or the divine help assigned by God.

To further unravel the four living creatures of Revelation that these cherubim represent, they were men who lived on earth, which is symbolized by the imperfect wings ("each of them had six wings"). Wings are a form of locomotion, which signifies earthly locomotion; six being imperfect while everything in heaven is perfect, and therefore, they all walk the earth. They are the ones that made the seal, or they started the events in the seal. For example, the first seal: "And I saw, and behold, a white horse, and he who was sitting on it had a bow, and there was given him a crown, and he went forth as a conqueror to conquer." All of the symbols represent England and the kings who conquered the whole known earth at that time. (The sun never fell on the English empire.)

Unlike the wings of the creatures in Ezekiel 1:6 that numbered four, these numbered six. As stated, the four living creatures in Ezekiel represent the four evangelists with the wings representing the lineage of Christ—Juda, the fourth tribe. Here the men are only signs and not highly elevated as the evangelists. However, God gave each his role, which is denoted by his symbol, i.e., a balanced scale for Dr. King, who was a living seal and whose role was his fight for justice. (The men who bared these seals will be given and discussed as they appear in the religious text.)

The eyes round about and within represent the fact that all eyes were on these men when their seals were being performed. They were studied closely and many things were written about them. Everyone knew them during their day; they all were and still are famous men. As in the case with King Richard, he was also a living seal, not only in all of Europe knew him, but also all of Arabia and Africa because of his quest to save the Holy City. As for Dr. King, since it was in our day, everyone knows the attention he has received. He was an international figure as all were.

The passage, "Holy, holy, holy, the Lord God almighty, who, was, and who is and who is coming," tells that the creatures announce the coming of God and His kingdom. This was done during the events in their seals. Each time one took place (seal), it announced the Second Coming of Christ. For example, King Richard's seal was the seal of conquest. It took many years for England to become a great nation, but King Richard was the most renowned king because of his efforts to recapture the Holy City, Jerusalem, from Arab occupation. Thus, the seal started with him and ran its course. History has never forgotten his heroic efforts; he was a sung hero in his own lifetime as were all of the horsemen, with the exception possibly of the fourth. Therefore, one understands that the seal event lasts in the hearts of many and continues long after the life of the horsemen. They are immortalized. Many eyes were on them and still are.

Another proof that favors King Richard as the first seal is the fact that he invented a type of crossbow, similar to the one invented in China. It was a weapon that helped with the type of war that was fought at that time. The weapon, with the long bow, allowed bowmen to exceed all existing firepower because of its quick loading ability, power, and accuracy. The two bows gave England's ground forces the firepower they needed to win many wars. As the kings of England's prowess at war enhanced, their territory enhanced. Hence, the old cliché, "The sun never sets on the English empire." The bow is a hint at King Richard being the first seal, along with the fact he physically went on the Third Crusade.

St. John also saw twenty-four elders seated around the throne of God. The twenty-four elders are the twelve apostles and the major and minor profits, men in both the Old and New Testaments.

These men are witnesses to God and performed the duties of heaven while here on earth. The prophets announced the will of God for Jews and guided them to God, in most instances back to God since the Jews fell away from God, prompting the call of prophets to redirect them back to God. The apostles were men of the New Testament whom Christ taught, men who also did God's will, carrying the news of the living God and saving men for God through salvation. And as mentioned in scripture, their audience was the gentiles mainly since the Jewish nation rejected Christianity, although, many Jews were converted to Christianity, as St. Paul was a convert through miraculous means.

We do not know anything about the order of heaven except that God sits on His throne and rules over heaven and earth. We don't know if there are colonels, majors, captains, and the like. We do know, however, that angels monitor the earth and report to God its condition and happenings, as the case with Sodom and Gomorrah. "I will go down and see whether they have done according to the cry that is come to me: or whether it be no so, that I may know (Gn 18:20).

It is felt by many theologians that the twenty-four elders will help Christ as a monitoring system set in place to rule the new earth. They would monitor its condition and circumstances and report it to Christ as the many angels and saints do to God the Father.

These men, through their sacrifices on earth, have earned a great place in heaven. This Christ has mentioned many times during His ministry. "The first will be last, and the last first." And those who do His will without seeking reward and are totally committed to saving souls will have a great reward in heaven. "Blessed are those that are persecuted and die for my sake, rejoice because their reward in Heaven is great (Lk 6:22-23).

The twenty-four elders around the throne are the ones who stood fervent by for both God and Christ; their reward is eldership and constant witness and aide to God.

In light of the foregoing, in essence, maybe it is good to follow God in simplicity at times, as the prophets did. If St. Paul had realized that God gave us the law to put peace on the earth and also human rights, then he would not have tried to stop the start of Christianity knowing that the Jews had fallen into idolatry many times in the past. This knowledge should have lessened his fear of Christianity. He should have observed Christ thoroughly and should have come to the realization that the man was authentic. There were too many miracles to dispute. He also would have understood that if he believed that God was with the Jewish nation, then nothing could overcome it. The Jewish nation still stands just as it did of old. Christianity did no harm to it.

It was not understood by man what God intended for the world. It was always told by the prophets and recorded in scripture that there would be a savior who would be rejected by His own: the Jewish nation and also the Arab nations. Isaac and Ishmael were brothers, but they were also to be a light to the Gentiles.

The Jewish nation thought that Christ would be a worldly savior, a savior that would free them from worldly oppression, an oppression that God sent because of their unfaithfulness and disobedience to Him. They could not comprehend that Christ had come to save the world, and the Jewish nation was only a vehicle He would use to accomplish His purpose.

This is not to take away from the Jewish nation because they were honored by God to be such a vehicle for Christ, the savior. Although they fell away many times, in their midst remained many devoted men of God, who obeyed Him to the letter.

It was God's plan to develop a nation that would lead the world righteously, a nation with whom He could have direct contact with in order to introduce His will. But the nation was so flawed that it fell many times into sin and even misled other nations who knew their story and saw the majesty and the power of God.

When the Jewish nation was strong, they converted many to God; and when they fell, they led many astray or they caused them to remain in the dark in sin, away from God. God intended for the Jewish nation to lead the way in terms of His righteous way. They fell short.

However, God knew that the Jews would fall short. Remember, His mind is not our mind. He knew that He would send Christ to save mankind. He used the Jewish nation as a focal point, an example. The nation was a vehicle that would know His will since they were visibly attuned to Him by the many miracles and the prophets who at times displayed miracles and were also visible. They could also see the chastisement of God upon them and the many things recorded by them from God.

Christ, as son of God, had a base in which He worked when He walked the earth to teach mankind his father's will. The people of earth had heard the message before and knew the people whom God had chosen. It was nothing out of the blue. There was a very defined history, and at the nation's peak all renowned persons wanted to see the Jewish nation, even the queen of Sheba (Sol, III Kings 10:1-7).

Therefore, one can see that the Jewish nation still stands. It still thrives because God made a promise to Abraham that it would. However, Christ is the central point. He has taken His rightful place as "Lord of Lords and Kings of Kings" as scriptures recorded many years prior to His coming.

Judaism is not discordant, but has evolved. This evolution has to do with the solidarity of the Trinity. God is Christ and Christ is God; they cannot be separated. Therefore, Christianity evolved from Judaism. Some people pray to God the Father, and some to Christ, and others to the Holy Spirit.

In whatever manner this is taken, there will never be a stronger gesture of love than the sacrifice that Christ made for the world. Through His sin offering of suffering and death, man is reconciled back to God the Father, our creator.

St. Paul, as a devote Jewish minister, put his soul in jeopardy by physically condemning or cruelly chastising the early Christian Church because the end result of such could have been many deaths by his hands. God said, "Thou shalt not kill."

Although Paul understood that God had chastised the Jews many times in the past for leaving His laws, Paul was probably afraid of Christianity as not being authentic, or of God. Instead of chastising the early Christians, he should have preached harder his point, leaving the decision to the listener as his free will to decide. He had a perfect command of scripture and knew all the writings, especially the Ten Commandments, one in particular, "Thou shall not kill."

God, the maker of mankind, does not interfere with man's free will, but rather gives all the freedom of decision. Man is left to choose the course he wants to follow, knowing that God has given him a conscience to discern right from wrong.

However, the lesson was a divine lesson for St. Paul because he was saved by Christ's intervention. St. Paul physically met Christ in the spirit realm. This meeting made St. Paul one of the greatest, if not the greatest biblical writer of all. Where would he be if God had not intervened? We all are richer for his encounter with Christ.

There have been many theological debates concerning Judaism versus Christianity. It is the discretion of the reader to validate each tenet.

As men, far too many fear when it comes to doing the work of the Divine, which is helping men reach perfection. Too often confusion results when men try to put their own stamp of approval on things. Working with God as a servant is to do what He says, using scripture as a guide because it also is Divine since it is also of God.

The twenty-four elders are the men who walked this earth calling men to God. Explaining who and what God is, giving mankind the promises of God, which sums up salvation if mankind keeps His commandments, is really the work of the prophets, Christ, the apostles, and modern men of God.

Possibly, there are many elders in heaven. Christ alluded to this when He spoke about St. John the Baptist. "There is none greater born of woman than he, but in Heaven there are greater than he." However, they are special to earth since they saved so many souls for God. They walked this earth timelessly and courageously for this end, giving all of themselves. Their places as elders were dearly earned and well deserved.

CHAPTER 5

THE SCROLL

In chapter 5, God holds a scroll sealed with seven seals. Seven represents a perfect earthy number, or a number that symbolizes God's hand or will for us, the inhabitants of this earth. Seven was used because it took seven days to create the earth; the seventh day God rested. As opposed to the number 12, which is designated for heavenly concerns and discernment, seven is for earth. God the Father rules in heaven as scriptures tells, but Christ will rule the earth. It is His domain and given to Him by the Father. Remember, we are talking about one being with three entities, the Trinity. Christ, who is God, is given all power over the earth.

It is argued by many that Christ came to not only save humanity but also test the flesh that was created, to feel the ordeals that the flesh encounters without the perfection of the Holy Spirit. This thought is understood because Christ's mission was to conquer the flesh, proving that a true, quality life is easy to obtain. When I say quality life, I mean a godly life free of sin or nearly free of major sins. Therefore, it is easy to misconstrue His mission as one of a test.

Christ said, "Accept me and learn from me, for my yoke is easy and my burden is light" (Mat. 11:28-30). There is nothing hard about obtaining salvation. All that is needed is to do as Christ did, say what He said, and love as He loved. He is the way to salvation. Christ not only opened the gates of heaven by His death on the cross, He also showed us how to live to gain it. If we would use His pattern, we should gain eternal salvation and also have a good life on this earth.

God did not intend for man to live in the manner that we are living now. He created the earth perfect and everything on it perfect. Adam's sin lost this perfection for us. Now man is imperfect and in sin. God, from the beginning, developed a plan to save mankind. It was a total plan that would put things right again and would allow Him to restore a beautiful world for man again, a world God intended for man in the beginning, a world of perfection.

God in His perfect state knows the temptations that we face and knows the flesh is made weak through indulgence. We are creatures of habit. This is the reason why many times in the Old Testament, God criticized the priests, scribes, and Pharisees for not instructing His people. Without that instruction, the Jews erred and were drawn into a spectrum of sin, thereby entrapped by sin. Therefore, God wants us to be knowledgeable of all the ills that the earth holds for us and to steer clear of them. Adam wanted knowledge; therefore, we have to learn everything in order to survive in this world.

The Holy Spirit held the earth in perfect perfection at the onset, when Adam and later Eve were on earth. The two were innocent, or free of sin, because they did not know what sin was. Like a child they were innocent. No habits could be formed because their flesh was pure; the Holy Spirit would not let habits take hold. They could not be harmed nor get ill because the Holy Spirit tended them. But when they ate the forbidden fruit, or sinned, God took the Holy Spirit away from them. They had disobeyed God's commandment of not to eat the fruit of knowledge. It was their choice; therefore, they had to learn everything to survive in the world.

They had to learn how to heel themselves when they got sick because the Holy Spirit would not heel them, they had opted for knowledge. Food was provided for them, they were shown what was good and it was plentiful. That also ended, they opted for knowledge; therefore, they had to learn what was good and how to cultivate it. They had to learn everything to survive on earth, the Holy Spirit was no longer a ready help for them. It was their punishment and is also ours as their descendants. They also obtained death from their folly because now, after sin, they were not perfect and they would die—their curse.

Since Christ saved the earth by His sacrifice of life, both devote mission and death, He is endeared by the Father who really cares about the welfare of His creation. We all have things that we have made that we truly treasure. Think about it, everything about the universe lives. It is very precise and extremely beautiful, a true work of art. Let no one be deceived, God is extremely proud of His creation. Thus, when Christ saved mankind, all power was given to Him, complete dominion over the earth.

Therefore, we have the number 7 symbolizing the number of days it took to complete the Creation with all of its minute details. This whole symbolism was assigned to Christ.

A strong angel asked who could open the scroll. "And I saw a strong angel proclaiming with a loud voice, who is worthy to open the scroll, and to break the seals thereof? And no one in heaven, or on earth, or under the earth was able to open the scroll or to look thereon."

From the beginning of time, God told man that He would send His son Jesus to save man from destruction, imperfection, and wickedness. At the same time, God knew that He would also end man's system on earth. This system was gained after years of man's punishment for Adam's sin, his punishment being to toil and labor on earth, an earth that was imperfect now because of Adam's sin (Gn 3:17).

Initially, man had no toils on earth because God held it in perfection as stated. But with Adam's sin, the perfection was lost and man had to go it alone. As he gained knowledge, which he chose over the Holy Spirit, he improved his life from the Stone Age to iron, all the way to the present. All ages are still imperfect. Thus, God knew He would end and restore His world to what He wanted in the beginning for man. At the end, He would have men who will have proven that they appreciate His world and are willing to abide by His laws and are ready to live in paradise in peace, harmony, and love—men who have passed God's test and have gained eternal life.

The scroll is a plan for this culmination of man's system, with only God knowing it in detail. It can be thought of as a blueprint with all the fine details for accomplishment. No one but God knows the blueprint. This is because He drew it up more or less. More or less because many things that happened are by man's hand with God being totally conscious of it. But again, many things are still affected by Him, or should I say, resolved or put straight by Him.

The culmination plan fits into God's overall plan, which was drawn up at the beginning. God, with His omniscient mind, knew that man would fall into sin; therefore, He made plans to save man from sin. As He molded man in clay, He paused upon the completion of the molded form to consider man's life. In a short span of time, the total life of man was shown to God by the Holy Spirit. Upon completion of the vision, God decided to bring man into life. This I was shown in a vision.

Part of the plan for man was to establish culture so that Christ could be sent. Without a culture to record His events, Christ would find it harder to establish a base. Bringing Christ on the scene with uncivilized men would be like throwing peals to swine. A well-defined culture, one that was basic at first, and could grow, would suffice. We have that first great culture in the Egyptian empire.

The Egyptians are still marveled at by all mankind even to this day. Their culture was the pinnacle of the ancient world. They were far advanced in engineering, farming, and society. The feats they accomplished still stands today for all mankind to marvel at. One, the pyramids at Giza are a wonder of the world.

Earlier, in preceding paragraphs, I mentioned that the numbers seven and twelve are Divine numbers. Another Divine number is 30. As a proof of God's existence and to show His hand or inspiration on the pyramid project, they were placed or built at thirty degrees latitude and thirty longitude. This is no coincidence. It is a signature from God to let the world know that He raised Egypt to the power it was.

As such, the pyramids at Giza are proof that God exists. In scripture, St. Paul tells us that God raised Egypt (Rom 9:17). The pyramids, the ones at Giza, are a testimony to His great power and existence. God endowed the Egyptians innate knowledge and a mastery of civil engineering and architecture. Some of there feats still have not been discovered as to how they were done. Only God could endow such mental prowess.

To qualify the above as being accurate and to show further the great and awesome power of God, if we were to extend the longitude to the next thirty degrees, we would be in Louisiana, near the area where I am from. And also a story that goes with me and that area. And if we would extend the longitude to the next thirty degrees east, we would be in Guadalupe Island.

What is being shown by God is that the pyramids were built by His inspiration, and the next thirty degrees east tells how I would deliver that message to you and other things. The next thirty degrees longitude east caps the sign that God placed because the site is named after a very famous visit by the Blessed Virgin Mary, the mother of Christ, who came to save the world. It is a culmination of the whole sequence from culture to Christ.

The whole manifestation is a definite proof of the existence of God. No one who knows scripture and has studied the word of God and understand logic can deny that this whole manifestation is not a coincidence or dreamed up by my imagination. It tells its own story by symbolizing the divine number 30, mission on the longitudinal thirtieth parallel and shifting the latitudinal thirty degrees until the story is complete at Guadalupe. Could any man do such?

To finish the symbolism and to dramatize the event, there is another number symbolized: the number 3. The number 3 symbolizes the Trinity, the Godhead. The Trinity is the three persons in God. Everywhere in the Bible where God is being symbolized, the number 3 is used. Three crossed on Calvary, Christ asking Peter three times to feed His sheep, Christ falling three times on His way to be crucified. All these symbolized that it happened to not only Christ but each person of the Trinity. There are three giant pyramids at Giza sitting at thirty degrees latitude and thirty degrees longitude.

What I am trying to show is that God actually exists and has shown Himself through mighty works in the Creation, which should give us a mighty faith in Him. God is real and every line in the scripture is true and real and will come to pass.

In writing this book, I had to ponder much on writing the foregoing and other text coming up, which is more dramatic because those who believe just on faith is a beautiful, immaculate thing. But so many can be saved if they read this book and understand the logic that is put before them. They also will believe in God to thus order their lives accordingly.

Now we have concrete proof that God exist, and as you read the pages of this book, I will show you more proof that God left for mankind, proving His existence. The foregoing only scratches the surface, but I don't want to dwell too long. There will be other books to detail many of the proofs I have tendered in this book, a dramatic but small start.

God also raised other cultures, another of God's cultures and empires were the Babylonians. This is told also in scripture. "Thou art a king of kings: and the God of heaven hath given thee a kingdom, and strength, and power, and glory" (Dn 2:37). This was told to king Nabuchodonosor, king of Babylon, by Daniel the profit. The king had a dream that none of his wise men could interpret. The king was very perplexed by the dream and had ordered all the wise men killed because they could not interpret the dream. Daniel was brought in to the king to interpret his dream, and he told the king his interpretation in the foregoing passage.

God raised Babylon as a great kingdom to subdue the Jews and end their freedom in the land that was given to them by God. They had sworn to a mighty covenant that they would obey God's law and not transgress any of His decrees or laws. They failed to keep their end of the covenant; therefore God raised Babylon to end them. This is shown to show that God indeed caused mighty kingdoms to exist for His own purposes and to further explain that Egypt was indeed God inspired.

Another passage in scripture that explains the fact that God raised Babylon is this: "A large eagle with great wings, long-limbed, full of feathers and of variety, came to Libanus and took away the marrow of the cedar. He cropped off the top of the twigs thereof and carried it away into the land of Chanaan, and he set it in a city of merchants" (Ez 17:3-4). This prophecy told by Ezekiel also tells that Nabuchodonosor was brought into existence to achieve God's will, that being the destruction of the Jews for all their waywardness.

The Babylonian empire was also great. It was known for its beauty and splendor, along with its evils and corruption of souls. I guess you'd say, how could a culture such as Babylon be raised by a God who is holy? Even today when sinful pleasure is thought of, Babylon is used as a theme. But unlike Egypt, it passed completely out of existence into the abyss, never to be seen again.

In the case of Babylon, God used evil to destroy evil. The evil that was done by Babylon was not as great as the Jewish nation because the Jewish nation was given the law to live by and made a covenant with almighty God to keep holy. They knew God through His intercession: first by Himself personally, then by the judges and prophets, especially the prophets who would work miracles in their sights, proving that God was with them. They knew the law, the Babylonians didn't; they were pagans, ignorant of God.

As our creator, God the Father went through great pains to bring mankind into the fold after Adam and Eve sinned. He conceived mighty plans with the greatest being the mission of His son, Jesus Christ. Jesus, being part of the Trinity, God made Him man—a man who overcame the ways of the flesh and was crucified as atonement for sin. Christ saved all humanity by His suffering and death on the cross. Through it all—the pains of nation rearing, sending many men to instruct human kind, and finally His son's anguish and death—this should indicate that God has a very profound love for mankind. It is displayed by countless instances and portrayed in holy scripture many times.

Jesus is the only person who could open the scroll for two reasons. First, He is of the divinity. Second, He is the one who saved the world by His death as an offering for sin and was totally worthy of knowing the plan since His role was such. His teaching and preaching lead men to God once the curse of sin was lifted by His death (Gn 3:17). Notice, although heaven was reopened by Christ's death, man still had to know how to live his life in order to be saved. This Christ taught as a fulfillment of the law. "I came to fulfill not to change the law" (Mt 5:17). The laws that we should live by as true children of God were given to Moses.

Therefore, we can see that the scroll can be understood as a complete plan by God to end man's system on earth and also to end the devil's hold on man, which is the most important thing, and to establish paradise once again with Jesus having complete dominion over it. The Trinity would be with man for eternity. Yes, someone was found to open the scroll. This someone was Jesus Christ, which is clearly proven by verse 6: "And I saw, and behold in the midst of the throne and of the four living creatures, and in the midst of the elders, a Lamb standing, as if slain, having seven horns and seven eyes, which are to seven spirits of God sent forth into all the earth. And he came and took the scroll out of the right had of Him who sat upon the throne. And when He opened the scroll, the four living creatures and the twenty-four elders fell down before the Lamb, having each a harp and golden bowl full of incense, which are the prayers of the saints."

Christ is symbolized as a lamb, meaning that He was slain for our sins and had overcome sin and death to prove that He was the Son of God and worthy to open the scroll. The seven eyes represent that He alone can look upon the seals and open them. The seven horns represents God's kingdom, which was opened by the death of Christ.

Also, Christ protects God's new kingdom as a he-goat protects his flock with His horns and as their leader. This is known by the passage where the seven horns and eyes are explained through "a Lamb standing, as if slain, having seven horns and seven eyes, which are to the seven spirits of God sent forth into all the earth." This is a reference to God's church, or His people. The number 7 means earthly perfection. This is why seven is used for all of God's earthly perfections: seven churches, seven golden candle sticks, etc., as explained. After Christ opened the scroll, all in heaven and earth began to rejoice and give praise to God.

Since the fall of man, all in heaven have been looking down to earth, praying for the inhabitants to come through the tribulation, or through Satan's wrath on the earth. They rejoiced over Noah, also Abraham, and of course the highest rejoicing was when God became man and dwelt with men. Heaven rejoiced over all of this because salvation for man was at hand. This was the ancient promise of salvation, and all heaven rejoiced when it was accomplished. All knew that those worthy of being with God would be saved. Christ would open heaven for them. They could be with their brethren on earth and enjoy an eternal brotherhood of peace.

Hence, we can see why it is written that all in heaven rejoiced when Christ opened the scroll. It was Christ who made the ultimate sacrifice, or offered Himself as a sin offering for all mankind. He was worthy to become the judge of mankind, a mankind He loves dearly. "No greater love a man has for a friend than to give his life for him" (Jn 15:12-13).

The scroll was also symbolic of Gods will for man. Christ was the only man holy and just enough to carry the will of God through; without Christ, salvation for man would not have been accomplished. The same love that Christ has for man is manifested by all in heaven as recorded by their rejoicing for Christ's successful mission.

"Worthy art thou to take the scroll and to open its seal; for thou wast slain and hast redeemed us for God with thy blood" (Rv 5:9). This passage sums up the narrative and is fully descriptive of why Christ was the only one who could rule over the earth—because He knew God the Father's will for it. However, Christ did not know the exact time for the end. This is known only to God the Father. The role of overseer of the earth and also the end was placed in the hands of Christ, the judge of all who ever lived on it.

CHAPTER 6

THE FOUR LIVING SEALS

For a better understanding of the four living seals, I will equate them to other parts of the Bible where the end is predicted. By doing so, you will see how each part fits into place. It also shows the existence and greatness of God since each person who was shown visions of the end existed, or lived, many years apart. Daniel did not know St. John and St. John did not know Daniel. St. John may have been told of Daniel's writings, which probably didn't make sense to him. Probably, after the vision St. John had, there still was no equation to Daniel's vision unless God revealed it to St. John.

The two principle participants who the end was shown are Daniel and St. John as cited above. Their visions are different on the surface but upon close inspection, you can discern that their visions of the end are like pieces of a puzzle. When both are placed together, you get a complete picture. Each complements the other, and they show the whole story.

A schema is shown for each in chapter 7 to depict what was conveyed to both St. John and Daniel and should visibly depict the four living seals in Revelation—St. John's four living creatures in Revelation and Daniel's four beast in the book of Daniel. All are the same but are parts that have to be pasted together to tell the complete story, or placed together to be understood.

Revelation chapter 6, "The Seven Seals," is very important because it gives a sequence of time and events elapsing before the Second Coming of Christ. It is done by the opening of the seven seals. Remember, Revelation does not take place all at once but rather the end is told by St. John as being time-sequenced events beginning with, for St. John's revelation, the first seal, who is King Richard. King Richard began the plan for the end in Revelation when his life was lived.

The first seal: "And I saw that the Lamb had opened the first of the seven seals, and I heard one of the four living creatures saying, as with the voice of thunder, 'Come'. And I saw, and behold, a white horse, and he who was sitting on it had a bow, and there was given him a crown, and he went forth as a conqueror to conquer."

The bow and the crown represent the kings of England, and when taken in conjunction with the description of the creatures in Revelation 4:6-8, one sees that the symbol of the first creature was a lion, which was the symbol of the king of England, especially Richard Plantagenet or Richard the Lionheart. England went forth and conquered the whole known world; her might was not surpassed for many years and her kings ruled many people.

In reference to the bow, it was King Richard who invented a type of crossbow similar to the Chinese because they had invented one long before the Europeans. Although the long bow was a weapon that revolutionized warfare at that time because the bow had good power and could be easily aimed with deadly accuracy and fired rapidly, the crossbow also played an important roll. The fact that King Richard invented a similar crossbow, which was used by English armies, distinguished him from other Kings. Thus we have a bow was given to him.

The white horse represents race. The first and third horses in the first four seals represent a particular race of men symbolized by the color white for Caucasian, and black for Negro. The second is red, which reflects a race but is not the actual color of the race, but rather its national flag. The fourth-seal horse has nothing to do with race but signifies an individual, as all of the first four seals were men who lived on earth.

The first seal's horseman is King Richard the Lionheart as stated earlier because first, he was one of the kings that helped solidify England being the offspring of an English father, Henry II, and a French monarch. Secondly, King Richard satisfies the biblical symbol by being known widely for his efforts in the Crusades. That effort made him famous, more so than any other king, especially to Christians. All eyes were on him, and he is still remembered for his courageous efforts.

King Richard had miraculous events recorded about him by writers. When he met the Muslim armada off the shore of the Holy Land, it was said that King Richard stood fearless on the bow of his ship with literally thousands of arrows flying past him. Many said they couldn't understand why an arrow did not strike him. Of course, he had that nature, and this is how he died, eventually. Ironically, King Richard died by a single arrow aimed at him while he was putting down an insurrection by one of his nobles. He ill-timed deflected the arrow with his shield and was struck in the neck by it. Although it was partially deflected, he died of the resulting wound.

It was also recorded that King Richard was a devout Christian, who attended mass regularly and gave much to the church. The Crusade alone was costly. Most of his own wealth was spent for the Crusade.

Many theologians think that the first seal is also symbolic of Jesus because He is known as the conqueror of the sins of the world. This could be true. However, it is stated that Christ opened the scroll, meaning the events of the seal are distinct from Him until it is stated that He will appear at the end on a cloud. Nothing is symbolic of Christ as the seals are actual events that happened on earth with certain individuals and are integral with the events they represent. This is the reason they are called the four living seals. The men actually lived, with one still living on earth, the fourth.

The second seal: "And when He opened the second seal, I heard the second living creature saying, 'Come.' And there went forth another horse, a red one; and to him who was sitting on it, it was giving to take peace from the earth and that men should kill one another, and there was given him a great sword."

The red horse of this seal represents Japan, "the Land of Rising Sun." It was Japan that took peace from the earth when she entered into World War II. Until she entered, the war was only in Europe, with Germany fighting Russia and daily bombarding England. The rest of Europe was taken, but when Japan entered the war, war circled the globe. When taken in conjunction with the description of the living creatures, which the second was a calf, it becomes clear that this seal is connected with Japan because of pagan worship. Later we will see that she is the bear that stood to one side.

There has never been a war that has touched so many countries and killed so many men. The reference to the calf suggests the Japanese religion, which is mainly Buddhism and does not believe in God but is pagan in nature. The calf is a symbol of idolatry, just as the golden calf that the Jews made while Moses was on the mountaintop with God. The calf is given as the description of the second living creature and further explains the second seal as being pagan in nature. The other description is that of the horse, which is red, the color of the Japanese flag, the rising sun.

The real reason for the war was Japan had become a powerful nation and wanted the United States to recognize her as such. The United States didn't; she regarded Japan as a second-rate country, and her citizens the same. The United States didn't let her expand her navy or armies. The United States controlled her. Japan wanted to be a powerful nation, and this could only be done by expansion of territory, which the United States hampered. Japan was an island and didn't have the natural resources needed to sustain her. Expansion, she felt, was imperative for survival.

Although Japan needed to expand to be a world power, she was reluctant to take on the United States. Only one man fought a tireless battle for war with the United States. His name was Tojo Hideki. The Japanese war cabinet and its parliament were split on the controversy of war with the United States. Tojo at the time was a renowned army general in the war cabinet. He single-handedly argued for war with the United States and slowly gained support. All felt that the United States was too powerful for them to win a war against, coupled with the fact that they were in a war with China over Manchuria, which they were winning. However, Tojo pressed on stating that the United States could be beaten.

What sealed the fate of war was when the prime minister of Japan, Konoe Fumimaro, resigned under the intense pressure. Tojo was relentless at him. Now that the prime ministership was open, the question of war loomed. The emperor of Japan, Hirohito, decided for whatever reason to push for Tojo to fill Konoe's place as prime minister. And after Tojo won the post, the question of war was sealed. If it wouldn't have been for Tojo's unyielding, tireless efforts, the Second World War would never have taken place, or better stated, the Second World War would have been confined to Europe. A sleeping giant was surely awakened.

The symbolism for Tojo goes like this: red horse symbolizes the flag of Japan, the rising sun, his country. Another symbol, the passage, "giving to take peace from the earth," means the whole earth was at war because of his efforts. Another symbol, the passage, "a great sword was given him," represents Tojo being a samurai, all of whom were given a katana, a sword of honor; and when placed with Daniel beasts, the bear standing to one side, Japan being a giant on her hemisphere, it gets clearer. When the historical facts are added, the whole picture is painted for all eyes. (Daniel's four beasts will be discussed in the next chapter.)

Next came the third seal. "And when He opened the third seal, I heard the third living creature saying, 'come' And I saw, and behold, a black horse, and he who was sitting on it had a balance in his hand. And I heard as it were a voice in the midst of four living creatures, saying, 'A measure of wheat for a denarius, and three measures of barley for a denarius, and do not harm the wine and the oil.'"

The black horse represents the black race, and the person who sat upon the horse had a balance in his hand. The balance represents justice, which is the symbol of the U.S. court system. At this point in time, there was no justice for the black man and other minorities. The person on the horse brought justice to the world because by his efforts, black men where freed all over the world. They gained first-rate citizenship, thereby justice was granted to them. All four living seals can be linked to Daniel's vision of the revelation in chapter 7 and the beast Daniel saw.

"A measure of wheat for a denarius, and three measures of barley for a denarius, and do not harm the wine and the oil." Every passage is a piece of the puzzle that explains the event and who that particular seal was, the personage. They are clues to who that person is. If we were to analyze the passage of the wine, corn, and the oil as to when it was used throughout the Bible, we would find that it is used when captivity and slavery is present (Joel 1:10, Jer. 31:12, Ez. 3:15, Is.

2:19, 2 Es. 13:5). In Joel 1:10 the symbol the corn, the wine, and the oil is used to denote clergy. It makes the demonstration stronger because it states clearly it is meant for the priest or clergy. However, it is as mentioned when slavery is mentioned in the Bible. Many times you will find stated in this book that the Bible is not a book that is arbitrarily written.

On the contrary, the Bible is strategically written to convey direct and hidden, symbolic meanings. By doing so, it could be understood that there is a greater being present and omnipotent than mere man because only a being of great caliber could manifest a writing that perfect and precise by the hands of mere mortal man. So precise and well executed that it is mind boggling, awesome. Only God could achieve this, thus it adds to the belief of His existence since we are told that He, and only He, can do such great feats.

In simplicity, what is being said is that at a certain point in the history of the world, there will be a black man, symbolized by the black horse. He will be part of the clergy, symbolized by the passages of wine, corn, and oil. He will fight for justice, symbolized by the balance in his hands; and all eyes in heaven and earth will be on him, symbolized by the eyes all round and about him as in St. John's vision of the creatures. What man in history can you think of that fits that bill other than Dr. Martin Luther King Jr.?

The symbol of the corn, the wine, and the oil is proven as a sign for the clergy in many books of the Bible, but for our purpose we will use the book of 2 Esdras 5:11 and 13:5, respectively. "Restore ye to them this day their fields, and their vineyards, and their olive yards, and their houses: and the hundredth part of the money, and the corn, the wine, and the oil." (The Jews were returning from slavery.) "Tithes of the corn, of the wine, and of the oil, the portions of the Levites (priests)." These two passages were used in conjunction with slavery and the clergy. As explained, the symbols of the Bible never change and stay consistent. Here the symbols of the corn, wine, and oil are used to denote both slavery and clergy and use thusly when the two are highlighted. One more, Deuteronomy 18:4. "The first fruits of also the corn, of the wine, and of the oil" (as portions for the priests of Israel). Therefore, it is used for Dr. King's seal to denote both he as clergy and an era of slavery.

All of the four living seals have the same symbolism, and when laid before you that way, you will know them, as everyone during their time. And after knowing them because they are very famous men, they are easily discerned. A child can fathom it.

At this seal's point in history, black people were poor and some were starving. If you were to look back in history, Dr. King took Robert Kennedy through the Mississippi Delta country to show him the squalor of the black people. It was said that Mr. Kennedy wept at the sight. He commented that he did not know that people in the United States were living in such a poor condition while the country sent millions of dollars for relief overseas. After that trip, giant steps were made to help the black and other poor people in the United States.

The forth seal is the seal that we are presently in. It is the pestilence seal. If we where to realize that there where many natural disturbances recorded from the year 1980 until now, than we can see that we are truly in the pestilence seal. There has been no point in the history of man where year after year, from one season to the next, there are major catastrophes—earthquakes, floods, tornadoes, blizzards, plagues, volcano eruptions, etc. Throughout history there were major disturbances, many of a great magnitude, but not with the frequency like our present time.

The fourth living seal: "And when he opened the fourth seal, I heard the voice of the fourth living creature saying, 'Come!' And I saw and behold a pale-green horse, and he who was sitting on it—his name is Death, and hell was following him. And there was given him power over the four parts of the earth, to kill with sword, with famine, and with death, and with the beast of the earth."

This is a very obscure seal, simply because versions of the Bible do not convey the fourth-seal horse as green. Rather, it is conveyed as pale in the Protestant Bible and sickly green in the Jewish Bible. Therefore, the symbol is obscured. However, the color is pale green, sickly meaning pale. Since I am thoroughly familiar with it, I will attempt to relay its meaning.

There is a person who is this seal living in the United States' southern region, the state of Louisiana. Presently, he is known not as a great person but rather as a person who is in the supernatural or affected by the supernatural. This is allowed by God so that the person could gain total recognition since he is not a King Richard, a Tojo, or a Dr. King. Remember, the four living seals must be known widely. It is the supernatural that gained him recognition. The details of how the super natural started and why will be left out to ward off trouble for certain parties since this seal is in the present.

The events of this seal started when this person was led to search for a marijuana field. When the field was found by this person, the events of the fourth seal began. A marijuana field gives off a light green hue when viewed from a distance and obscured. When he found the field, it was viewed as a light green hue or pale green, the color of the fourth-seal horse.

From that minor incident, many things were set into motion because many people use drugs in the United States and other countries. This person, as the others were, was set apart from mankind by God. They were wards of God, so to speak. The fourth was shown heaven when he was a child, thus is protected by God from his youth.

Since he is the last, he recorded all the others so that God's hand, or scripture, could be fulfilled. Just as Samson, the last judge for the Jews, he must be known to through light on the others and fulfill the prophecy or revelations.

Samson was given superhuman strength so that his might could be recorded and his mighty exploits and adventures could be remembered and told. He was the last and had to give credit to the rest as being wards of God. There is no reason for his superhuman strength except that it was and indication that God's hand was on him.

The fourth living seal, pestilence came in when this person or ward of God was subjected to all sorts of atrocities because of people's love for drugs. Since he is a ward of God, like Moses, Noah, and Abraham, God would retaliate with pestilence, earthquakes, floods, tornadoes, and the like. This seal person even showed the leaders of the United States signs from God to attest to his prophet status. He is a person who constantly hears from God.

What he tendered was a prophet's proof, which was prompted by God the Father Himself. He told the fourth-seal person to do so. It was a very simple task. Some believed and some didn't because it was too profound for some, and they thought they knew more about God than a person whom God has been with for only a quarter of a century. They are pompous to God.

Pestilence was also shown for even just scuffing at this person's work. This person, since he was subject to man's cruelty, tried to give a community program to the U.S. government so that he could work for God in peace, but was turned down. Major pestilence was sent because God wanted to see this person prosperous. Even inventions were turned down and God sent major catastrophes for each.

There were many signs given by God for this person's goodness and purity of heart, which were ignored by hordes of people. Only the righteous seemed to care about this person, to care about his plight—the righteous, the real children of God. Not known, many received great blessing for their help, whatever it was, and hordes are cursed to hell for their efforts to void this person of his efforts for humanity and generally his good life on earth. Many of that horde were people who were drug users. You see, many honor the code of drugs—a hidden code, a demon. God showed this man to be just and innocent, yet many where inhumane to him.

The pestilence seal carry many curses with it, not only the major catastrophes, but also things or diseases such as Aids and also a curse of a deadly drug—crack cocaine. This was sent because many tried to drive the personage of the fourth seal insane or break him, give him a nervous breakdown. Therefore, you can see the play on the name crack cocaine, a drug that takes many lives and leaves many void in its wake. Literally, thousands upon thousands are wasted to nothing, drug addicts, because this drug is very addictive.

Another was a curse on the young or youth of America. Gangs and designer drugs take their toll on them. The young black and Mexican portray manhood as gangsters and the young whites bury their brains on designer drugs that literally eat their brains. There was a saying on the fourth-seal personage that he was "no man and no brain." The youth of America bore the curse with distorted manhood, killing that is not a manly trait, no man and brains are being eaten away by designer drugs, no brain. A wise counselor, the fourth-seal mother, told him that blacks considered him as not being a man, and whites considered him as not being a brain. *Newsweek* carried an article addressing the fact that boys are falling way behind in academics. The war on drugs remains seesawing from year to year.

The forth seal is a very real seal. The personage of this seal was shown by God that he is indeed this seal. Only God could have conveyed it to him. On his own, he could not discern it because it is very complex to note. But once God showed or revealed it to him, he immediately understood. The personage of this seal is the only one of the seals to know what he is. The others only acted their seals out by living their lives and their personal challenges, not knowing that they were living seals of the Bible. As mentioned, the last is always given the task by God to announce the undertakings of God, qualifying the entire group who acted in the same vein.

As with the judges, Samson was given superhuman strength to accredit the entirety of the judges. Everyone could see Samson was not ordinary, thus of God. The same with the fourth living seal. Miracles in his youth were displayed in the form of mighty leaps while playing basketball, no one could physically jump that high. It was God's way of displaying His might and that the personage of this seal was real. He was given three mighty leaps by God in the presence of all in the audience; however, at different times or different games.

When you talk of drugs, one thinks of organized crime or the Mafia. God showed His might that this person or any other person in His family or friends should not be touched by them. In fact, oddly enough, the mob liked this person and at times would offer aid. This is also an indication of how God's hand was in it. Why should organized crime like this person? One reason is they knew that things got out of hand and it was not the person's real intent to put a damper on the Mafia.

The Mafia knew that this person's heart would never want to see anyone go to jail because of their wayward thinking. Just as Christ does not want to see people imprisoned, it is the same reason He asks that we visit and help those imprisoned. The world is wicked and many fall by the wayside. However, in an attempt to down this personage of the fourth seal, lies were told that the Mafia wanted him down. This was to achieve the evil doers' ends, knowing that people are very afraid of the Mafia. Yet because of God, His warning, the mob stayed steadfast to the personage of the fourth seal.

The four living seals are crucial to Revelation or the Apocalypse. Christ, when asked about the end, told of the pestilence before the end and that pestilence is found in the fourth seal, which is the pestilence seal. All of the first four seals were events on earth with the four horse riders (men) being the sole characters who started or headed the events. The eyes of the world were on them; they were and are still famous men. However, since we are in the fourth seal, it is very obscured or hard to discern. In reality, it is hidden in plain view because the pestilence is very pronounced. Even if the seal was not announced by the fourth living seal, the man who is portrayed as the pale green horse rider, the pestilence would be noticed.

God goes through great pains to bring man to the realization that He both loves him (man), and He wants the best for him (man). These events could have been kept under guise, but God shows them to mankind so that mankind will know what time it is. All who are presently living are given a chance to reconcile himself to God. In fact, all living beings were given that chance through the word, here the Bible. There is no secret, God exists and the world is ending. The time markers are there and personified by God's ward with all proofs.

Do you recognize the signs that God has given, or do you choose to ignore them and keep trekking down the same unrighteous paths, where many who lived before us have been on, knowing that all is lost if there is adherence to those wrong broad paths.

Chapter 7

Daniel's Four Beasts

Daniel's vision of the end can be discussed in terms of the four living seals. Daniel's vision is found in chapter 7 of his book, the book of Daniel. Note that Daniel's vision of the end is presented to show the continuity of both, thus proving the prophecy of Revelation and most importantly proving the existence of God because the two writings are hundreds of years apart but complement each other perfectly to such an extent that the two had to have been inspired by the Divine.

Daniel chapter 7:

> In the first year of Baltassar king of Babylon, Daniel saw a dream: and the vision of his head was upon his bed: and writing the dream, he comprehended it in few words: and relating the same of it in short, he said: I saw in my vision by night, and behold the four winds of the heaven strove upon the great sea. And four great beasts, different one from another, came up out of the sea. The first was like a lioness and had the wings of an eagle: I beheld till her wings were plucked off, and she was lifted up from the earth and stood upon her feet as a man, and the heart of a man was given to her. And behold another beast like a bear stood up on one side: and there were three rows in the mouth

thereof, and in the teeth thereof, and thus they said to it: Arise, devour much flesh. After this I beheld and lo, another like a leopard, and it had upon it four wings as of a fowl, and the beast had four heads, and power was given to it. After this I beheld in the vision of the night, and lo, a fourth beast, terrible and wonderful, and exceeding strong, it had great iron teeth, eating and breaking in pieces, and treading down the rest with its feet: and it was unlike to the other beast, which I had seen before it, and had ten horns. I considered the horns, and behold another little horn sprung out of the mist of them: and three of the first horns were plucked up at the presence thereof: and behold eyes like the eyes of a man were in the horn, and a mouth speaking great things.

St. John's four living creatures and the four seals were presented to Daniel in a different form. They were beasts or the kingdom where these men resided when their seals where being performed. The third beast is the only one that does not correspond with representing a kingdom; it relies on history to be disclosed because the third and fourth seals take place in the United States. These beasts further explain the four seals and help fit the pieces of the puzzle so that a clear picture can be discerned.

"The first beast was like a lioness and had the wings of an eagle." Here again, the lion symbolizes England. The following passage shows how the United States is born out of the English system. "I beheld till her wings were plucked off, and she was lifted up from the earth, and stood upon her feet as a man, and the heart of a man given to her."

The passage says that out of England came the U.S. of America, symbolized by the wings of an eagle that gave her citizens freedom. Her system of government, a democracy, was more humane. This is symbolized by the heart of a man being given to her. The United States was made a free nation when other nations were unjust and tyrannical to their citizens.

"And behold another beast like a bear stood up on one side: and there were three rows in the mouth thereof, and in the teeth thereof, and thus they said to it. 'Arise, devour much flesh.'"

Here, again, the second beast is the same as the second seal (red horse). The beast is Japan, and a bear is her symbol. The color red is equated to her flag, the rising sun. Note that Daniel saw that the bear stood on one side, which represents that Japan's power over her domain. She was a military might at that time. The passage, "And there were three rows in the mouth thereof, and the teeth thereof, and thus they said to it: 'Arise, devour much flesh,'" means that Japan started war against the United States, putting the whole earth into war since Europe was already at war with Germany.

The U.S. government is comprised of three branches—the executive, legislative, and judicial—thus the three rows of teeth. The fact that the bear stood up on one side indicates or suggests Japan's power over her domain or the most powerful nation in her hemisphere. She was told to devour flesh, meaning that she started World War II by attacking Pearl Harbor. This event started World War II, with many being killed by her forces throughout the war.

Also, the second seal, when placed with the second beast, helps to identify the rider. The second seal is red, the color of the Japanese flag, the raising sun. Also, the second beast stood on one side. Japan was the most powerful nation in her hemisphere, with the United States being the most powerful over hers. The symbols that really bring the picture up are the three rows of teeth—the three branches of our government. Those teeth tore through the United States.

The third beast: "After this, I beheld, and lo, another like a leopard, and it had upon it four wings as of a foul, and the beast had four heads, and power was given to it."

When taken in conjunction with the third seal (black horse), we see that they are the same. The third seal and the third beast represent a man; the third beast has the symbol of a leopard with the color explained as the color of the horse and explains the seal further because a leopard can also be black, as the third seal, the black horse. Note that no color was mentioned about the leopard, but the leopard is black because it corresponds to the third seal, which is Dr. King. This seal states that he has the face of a man. This equates to Ezekiel's evangelist; they all had the face of a man on one side. Therefore, the third seal was clergy.

Another reason for the symbolism of Dr. King is that third seal represents the fact that he stood for justice. Dr. King helped to establish justice throughout the world, not just the United States by his courageous leadership. Many used his method of peaceful demonstration borrowed from Mahatma Gandhi.

The four wings and the four heads mean four groups or organizations that identified themselves with the movement: the NAACP, Dr. King's organization; the Students Nonviolent Steering Committee; the Southern Christian Leadership Conference; and the Urban League.

The fourth beast, just as the fourth seal, is the most obscure of all the beasts in terms of equating back to its seal because it is the one in which we presently live in. Even the makeup is different from the others, as the other three are directly identifiable to Daniel's vision in terms of symbols equating to symbols.

For example, the first living creature was a lion; the first seal was a white horse, whose rider was given a crown to conquer. In Daniel's vision, the beast was like a lioness and had the wings of an eagle. Both are England and her kings or a certain king. The lion represents England, and many of England's emblems are lion symbols. The white horse, whose rider was given a crown to conquer, represents England, which conquered the whole world. The lioness with wings of an eagle is the United States born out of England, with the U.S. national bird being an eagle. This is why the wings were plucked off because the United States had not been born yet. Consequently, England had to exist first as the country of the first seal or after this happened, and then England gave birth to the United States. The symbol was a means of identification.

All the foregoing symbols are directly related to England and Japan; but in the fourth seal, the symbols do not equate as visibly to the fourth beast because the fourth beast is a symbol that is not a wild animal. It is the only one that is animated as such. Below is a schema of the equation between Daniel's vision: the four beasts, the four living creatures, and the first four seals.

beast   =   kingdom
living creature   =   symbolic Christian temperament
seal/horse   =   event

(Note the symbol = means equates or gives)

The foregoing schema is a pattern of how the two visions, Daniel and St. John, equate. They are like a jigsaw puzzle that when put together gives a picture, collectively, from the varied pieces that they link. Here, the greatness of God and the might of the Bible are displayed as these jigsaw pieces are abstracts from a supreme being who is communicating to man or rather to man's limited senses.

The first seal schema:

Daniel's first beast	=	lioness with eagle wings (England)
St. John's first living creature	=	lion (Ferocity)
first seal / white horse	=	crown to conquer (conquest)

The second seal schema:

Daniel's second beast	=	bear standing on one side (Japan)
St. John's second living creature	=	calf (pagan)
second seal / red horse	=	war (destruction)

The third seal schema:

Daniel's third beast	=	leopard (Strength)
St. John's third living creature	=	face of a man (Clergy)
third seal / black horse	=	Balance (Justice)

The fourth seal schema:

Daniel's fourth beast	=	ten horned beast (U.S.)
St. John's fourth living creature	=	eagle (keen Divine insight)
fourth seal / green horse	=	pestilence (destruction)

The fourth beast: "After this I beheld in the vision of the night, and lo, a fourth beast, terrible and wonderful, and exceeding strong, it had great iron teeth, eating and breaking in pieces, and treading down the rest with its feet: and it was unlike to the other beast which I had seen before it, and had ten horns. I considered the horns, and behold another little horn sprung out of the mist of them: and three of the first horns were plucked up at the presence thereof: and behold eyes of a man were in this horn, and a mouth speaking great things."

The ten-horned beast that Daniel saw has two meanings superimposed. First, as in the vision, the beast as seen is the U.S. government with her governmental structure. The ten horns are the bill of rights in the constitution. The three horns are the various branches, namely, the legislative, judicial, and executive branch. The horn with the eyes and mouth is the president of the United States, who speaks for the country. Just with that symbol, "a mouth speaking great things," we should discern that it must be a politician. Secondly, the ten-horned beast is also the actual physical military state of the country. Daniel saw the beast "eating and breaking in pieces, and treading down the rest with its feet." In this sense, Daniel sees all the wars that the United States engaged in, her many victories, and her military might.

The time sequence is placed at World War II, where the Unites State prevails. Since the start of the fourth seal, there were no major wars; therefore, this suggests the military might of the country during past wars. This was shown to Daniel for him to perceive the military might of the United States. This is also proven by the fact that the fourth seal is pestilence, where there are no major wars. There were a few military actions or skirmishes, but no prolonged wars, just famines, earthquakes, volcano eruptions, and other things that plagued the world. More importantly, the time sequence is placed at World War II because from that point on, ten presidents must serve before the start of the end. Logically, all countries of the world are old enough to have had more than ten head of states.

Now, it is not difficult to understand that the four beasts in Daniel's vision of revelation are connected to and further explains the four living creatures and the first seals, or conversely. Remember, there are many years that separate the two men; each vision has a different symbol, but they both tell the same message. The symbols are different yet similar and compliment each other.

This book, as mentioned before, is an effort to reveal to its readers that there is a supreme being who created this earth and has done everything that the Bible says He has done. It is an attempt to prove God's existence to those who don't believe and strengthen the belief in those who do.

God went through great pains to right mankind with himself. I once stated that we do not know the makeup of heaven, its government and worship practices, but we do know or have been told that there is perfect peace there and that there is a worship of God by the many beings who reside there. In essence, God wants us to be in accord with the beings in heaven so that we can be one complete, holy body, both heaven and earth. It is His will for His creation.

In the interpretation of Daniel's vision, Daniel was troubled and asked about the vision. It was not identified who did the interpretation, but the person gave the vision to Daniel briefly so that he may not be troubled. If he had given Daniel an interpretation in detail, Daniel would not have understood. Also, whoever the person was, he did not want Daniel to know the time of the end because God did not want it disclosed. This is why the ten horns' and the three horns' explanations were disguised or superimposed. He felt that Daniel would not understand, and it would trouble him more because he could not understand future cultures or civilizations and their governmental structures.

CHAPTER 8

THE FIFTH AND SIXTH SEALS

In the fifth seal, all those who were slain for the word of God began to ask God when they will be avenged. And they were given a white robe and told to wait a little longer until their brethren were slain like them.

This passage means that God's saints who will remain persecuted on earth must die like all will before He avenges them. In this seal, the slain saints will see what is happening on earth and will ask God when He will avenge them by destroying the earth. They will be ready for the new system that would follow the destruction of the earth.

The saints who were killed include all the men and women from the beginning of the church, the Jewish nation. The people who were slain even then fall into the category of the saints. That era, the judges and prophets, all fall into the same group as the Christians. They also where slain for God's word, they also were outstanding God-fearing men and women. And for their belief in a supreme being, they where slain. They died professing a deep faith in God Almighty, not Christ, but God the Father. Then, there are the countless many who were killed because they followed Jesus Christ's teachings.

Although the early Jews suffered for their faith, the greatest suffering came during the era of Christianity where literally thousands and thousands where savagely slain. Many met terrible deaths but did not lose their faith in Christ.

Christianity springing from Christ's teaching grew very rapidly. It is conceivably hard to realize why a new religion as Christianity survived, looking at it from a basic point of view. First, the Jews had endured much suffering by the hand of God for falling away from His laws. They had learned a clear lesson by paying a tremendous cost for falling away. Why did the new religion take hold of them by such large numbers? They knew that if they didn't follow the law, they could be cast again into slavery.

What took hold of all of the followers of Christ was the fact that all were dedicated preachers and teachers of His word, and they displayed the Holy Spirit wherever they went. To ensure that the teaching of Christ were from God, many great signs in the form of miracles where manifested. There was too much to the new religion; it was soothing to the ears and understanding of men—a message of love and forgiveness and a reward that could not be described in earthly terms for those who adhered to the new law and an even greater reward for those who carried or lived that word and died for it.

Yes, the beginning struggle was extremely intense, with many lives being gladly given. Even now lives are given for Christianity in faraway countries. Christianity encircles the globe as God said that it must before the end. The word will be preached to every corner of the globe, to the ends of the earth so that everyone can hear it. Everyone is given a chance to gain eternal salvation by hearing and living the word, everyone.

Remember, in simplicity, our stay on earth is just a test to see if we will obey God's commandments and decrees. Adam didn't; therefore, as his descendants, we must be tested as He was tested to see how we will fare, to see if we will choose God. All have to pass through this test. God, in a loving manner, also knows that the earth was going to be in a horrible state because through sin, the earth is defiled with nothing going the way it should as man is too fallible to keep this earth in perfect harmony. This is the reason that He places strong emphasis on helping each other by giving to the poor, clothing the sick, visiting the shut in, etc., because He deeply cares and does not want to lose anyone through the ordeals of earth the way it is now. There are deadly traps waiting for all who don't rely on God's help to pass this test.

All those who put a special effort to enlighten others to God and help with their fellow man's journey, God gives special privileges to. Since it is a test, His hands are more or less tied because He does not want to interfere. It is your choice, right or wrong, but for all the other things that can happen such as poverty, illnesses, isolation, etc., He bids that we help each other.

And when a person does the things that He (God) wants, they are highly rewarded. The ones who are slain for God's work will be rated higher than any other on the earth and rewarded accordingly. They are the ones that God is waiting for to fulfill their mission before He ends man's system on this earth and once again restore it to its initial luster. It will be a very glorious day; there will be nothing like it in the history of the world.

The sixth seal begins the end. Here begins the strife of the earth, which will take place in the seventh seal. God will turn away from the earth and will begin His retribution. But before He allows the earth to be harmed, He will make good His promise to Abraham that his seed will be great and take a great place in heaven, which begins chapter 7, the sealing of the spiritual Israel.

In the sixth seal are great signs that will take place before the beginning of the end. These signs are natural occurrences, but on a higher level, the first being a great earthquake. This earthquake may be the largest earthquake that has ever been recorded on earth. Of course, the location is not given but it will be one of the signs that will take place, thus marking the sixth seal.

The second great sign mentioned is the sun becoming black like sackcloth of hair. This great sign is disguised and really is a great volcano eruption. St. Helena was a good example of how black the skies will get with falling ash from that eruption. The time sequence is not given as to the spacing of these events, but they will be dramatic enough to cause great concern pointing to the end of the world being at hand.

Third, the whole moon will become red as blood. As mentioned above, the time sequence is not given. This event may be in conjunction with the volcano eruption as a natural condition for the moon, but heightens the effect because of the awesome eruption, which will make it look like a bad omen. The reader should understand that type of impact after a major catastrophe.

After the moon becomes red as blood, the stars of heaven will fall upon the earth. This event is not in the same time frame as the others. But it suggests or states that there will be a shower of meteorites, which will be great in terms of many of them falling in the course of a certain period. All of these signs will be dramatic, but many may not happen in one part of the world, but rather spread out over the world, as the pestilence seal is now spreading across North and South America, Africa, Europe, etc. The one in the sixth seal will be greater than these in magnitude and will cause great dismay.

The passage, "heaven passed away as a scroll that is rolled up," means that at this stage, because of atmospheric conditions, the sky will look unfamiliar. Notice that the passage goes on to say, "Every mountain and the island were moved out of there places." This in itself suggests that there will be great geological disturbances, which will cause a change in weather conditions, and the effect will be seen in the sky. The terminology heaven is used meaning sky. It is important to note that heaven is used interchangeably as being the sky and the actual tangible place where God resides.

The disturbances will be so great that the people on earth will have great fear and many will run about seeking a place they think is safe. The same occurs when an earthquake hits. The ground shakes violently, tumbling buildings over and breaking the pavement and the like, causing panic. Well, the same is true for this sign when the mountains and the islands are moved out of their places. This statement says that there will be a major shifting of the earth's surface, which will affect the above; therefore, tremors will be felt around the world.

CHAPTER 9

THE SEALING OF SPIRITUAL ISRAEL

In chapter 7, St. John saw an angel ascending from earth saying to the four angels who had the power to harm the earth and the sea not to do so until they have "sealed the servants of our God on their foreheads." And he heard that 144,000 would receive God's seal. These 144,000 servants would be descendants of Abraham or of the Jewish nation. Twelve thousand from each of the twelve tribes would be selected.

God had promised Abraham that He would make his seed a great nation. This was promised from the beginning, at the very first meeting between God and Abraham. From that time on, the promise of the Messiah was taking form.

As it is with God, Abraham was observed and even known by God before he was in his mother's womb. He possessed everything that God wanted man to be, but the most important thing of all, Abraham was obedient and totally humble to God's wishes, which in effect, is having the characteristic of faith. It was that faith that led Abraham away from the security of his countrymen to journey far into a land that was not familiar to him, but familiar only through a promise.

The promise is know today as the promise of salvation. This nation that God would raise from Abraham's loins would be the nation that would carry His word to all mankind, and eventually a son of that nation would be slain for the sins of all mankind. Since the seed was a cleansed seed, one that knew God and His wishes and blessed by God, it was esteemed enough to be a sin offering for mankind.

No one knows the make up of heaven, how God is worshiped, or how is sin atoned for if there is any sin there. I would gather that every being is in total obedience to God. But in scripture, we find that when Satan is released, even the elect of God purify themselves. With that we can see both the total evilness of Satan and also the fallibility of created beings since they purify themselves to ward of Satan's effects.

By using deductive reasoning, we can understand that there must be some type of ritual to purify oneself from Satan; therefore, there is a method of prayer in honor of God to achieve this. With that we can understand that all being must seek the protection of God and His holy host to ward off the deceiver of all, and that this system has to be manifested both in heaven and on earth. From this we get the total sacrifice of Jesus for all mankind. Seemingly, man was so far out of line with God that it would take a being of the Godhead to negate man sins.

Whatever the circumstances, however, praise and atonement is accomplished in heaven. The reality is that fact that Jesus Christ ransomed mankind back to God by His blood. The most profound thing is that Christ also used the opportunity to teach us about God, which could have also been part the ransoming effect. Whatever the heavenly scheme of things, we all are saved by the total gesture of love by God.

Christ was the promise of salvation. Not only did Christ come through the lineage of Abraham, but also in preparation of His coming, many holy men came to announce the one and only living God. These were the prophets that God chose to do so. These men were cleansed by God to carry their mission to completion.

Since the word was entrusted to this nation, it was a special nation to God because of the one man who was faithful enough to adhere to God's every wish. God truly loved Abraham for it and blessed both him and his seeds immensely, making any of Abraham children who also kept His word very special to Him.

The 144,000 are the direct descendants of Abraham, who like him were devoutly faithful. As Abraham, they both loved God and their fellow man and

73

adhered to the laws of God, which were given through the prophets and written by God for Moses. This is why there is a special ceremony for them. God will seal them on their foreheads for all to see that they are special to God.

The story of the Jews is in itself a very special story because it also tells how God through them taught primitive man many things from medicine to farming, quarantine and cleansing of sores and wounds, crop rotation, etc. Man did not know these things then. Some things were only used by the Jews until science was fully developed. In fact, many acres of futile land were made waste because of over farming. There was no crop rotation as far up until the sixteenth century.

In fact, God gave everything for the existence of man to the Jews. They had the choicest meats, fowl, and fish to eat. When God was with them, they lacked nothing. At their highest level, they were the envy of the countryside. Many came to see the splendor of Solomon. At times, however, the Jews were, as God terms it, "stiff necked people," who did not fully love or appreciate the God who was trying to make them a great nation. They were too sinful; therefore, He would scatter them to the ends of the earth by permitting them to be enslaved. This happened time after time.

They were a holy nation who knew God; they were not a people of the dark. They were tended by God Almighty Himself, yet they permitted themselves to fall short of the royal birth right and honor and fell into sin. More so, this is why God has special honor for those who remained true to Him. He will proudly knight them as true children of God.

As stated in my introduction, I said that I would offer proof to God's existence; and at this juncture of my book, I will offer another proof of the existence of God. When Adam sinned, God removed him from the Garden of Eden and told him that a woman would save mankind and that Satan would strike at her heel and she would strike at his head. The proof of the existence is the etching of the country of Israel. You will note that the whole country is in the shape of a foot, with a very profound heel pointing down.

This is the reason why God asked Abraham to move to that special land because it is etched for all mankind to see that the word of God lives. Ancient man could not discern this because he had no compass line to draw the outline of the continent. Modern man has the means and has drawn the outline of the continent, and we have a very distinct shape of a foot with a heel pointing down in a crushing blow. No one on this earth can say that they cannot equate the meaning of such from the biblical statement that Satan would strike at her heel and she at his head, to the actual shape of Israel as a foot with a very discerned striking heel, the etching of the very land where He placed Abraham (Gn. 3:15).

This proof is a very simple proof, but it is awesome and dramatic. It shows the complete and majestic power of God. The holy land was etched many millions of years before man ever existed on this planet. God, the creator, was aware of man at the start of Creation and even at that time He knew man's plight on earth and made complete provisions for that plight.

As with the Egypt proof, with the longitude and latitude parallels, the final or culminating piece stops in the state of Louisiana. Louisiana is also in the shape of a foot and this is the state where the fourth living seal lives. With that everything falls into place like a jigsaw puzzle; every thing is connected. It is connected because it was shown to the last living seal to write and explain that mystery. And since I reside in Louisiana, it is shaped like a foot to prove that what I am saying is true and for mankind to take heed to what I am saying about the Divine. It is a call by God that man should order his ways and turn to God before the end of time because the end of time is drawing near. (I first wanted the reader to sense I am the fourth seal before I would give it to all.)

There are other areas both in the United Sates and the world shaped in the form of a foot and heel, and if the story is known, they do relate to the fourth living seal. However, I will not explain them in this book because much of the story is known and to explain them here will detract from the main underlying purpose, the existence of God and His love for man. However, a few are given on the back cover. They also prove the existence of God.

As with every writer, there is a concern that the information that is presented is complete and concise for all readers to understand, especially the foregoing because it is of God and needs to be understood thoroughly. As the writer of this text, I ask for no honor because all this was shown to me and given to my understanding to convey to you. Many have contempt for me even now and many more will have, it is the way of erring, wayward mankind to be such. But understand me well, it is God who has a deep, never-ending love for His creation, man, and it is He who makes provision for each and every one of us to be saved. The sending of Christ, God's son, was a gesture of love that cannot be compared with. And daily, God suffers insults to His very being because He is extremely holy and righteous. Yet, He endures because He has the plan to save mankind in the end.

After the sealing of Israel, those in heaven clothed in white garments cried, "Salvation belong to our God who sits upon the throne, and to the Lamb." Those clothed in white were many other people from all nations who had kept God's word and had received heaven for their reward. This is given to us in verse 13: "And one of the elders spoke and said to me, those who are clothed in white robes, who are they and whence have they come? And I said to him, 'My lord, thou knowest,' And He said to me, 'Those are they who have come out of the great Tribulation, and have washed their robes and made them white in the blood of the Lamb. Therefore, they are before the throne of God, and serve Him day and night in His temple, and He who sits upon the throne will dwell with them."

This tells of the many non-Jewish people who have proven to be worthy to be with God. They have lived their lives in accordance with the laws of God. A great multitude knows the law, but some didn't but yet were saved because the law was written in their hearts. You see it's by your heart you are saved. These souls both loved God and their fellow man and came through the tribulation or test that God will have let happen to man. They lived the way God wanted man to live, the way He wanted Adam to live. By then all is at peace. Christ can live with man in a perfect world now that the unfits have been removed from the midst of the righteous; paradise has been restored.

After the death of Christ, attention turned to the gentiles, although throughout His ministry, Christ used the gentiles as examples of divine brotherhood. To the Jews, the gentiles were considered debased and heathens. St. Peter's fervent work as an apostle of Christ opened the realm of Christianity to all nations of the world.

Before the Acts of the Apostles, the Jews were told that the Gentiles were to take a great place with God (Is 42:6), but until St. Peter's vision in Acts

11:1-18, they were not baptized into the Christian Church. The sacred word of God was with the Jews only until St. Peter was made aware of God's will for the gentiles.

God, through His will, had chosen the Jews to instruct and convert as a vessel to contain the savior of the world; they had to be knowledgeable of God and walk in His light before Christ could be sent. In other words, they had to be cleansed. The gentiles, however, were never really excluded from God's salvation. In fact, the readying of the Jews was the groundwork for the salvation of the world.

Through them the world could see that God really existed as the Jews claimed, and since other nations of people were always living around the Jews, they too came in contact with God's laws and, of course, the customs that He laid out for the Jews (Is 60:3-9). This is the reason why God told the Jews to let others live among them, so that they could see the light of God and be saved.

Christ used the Gentiles as an example to illustrate kindness and good Christian works when He preached salvation to the Jewish nation. But the invitation to gentiles was extended long before Christ's ministry. God the Father made mention of the gentiles in various books of the Bible in the Old Testament (Is 60:3, Is 11:10, Gen 49:10, Mal 1:11). There too He made mention that the gentiles will also be added to the kingdom of heaven if their life works were pleasing to God. Although He said it in a way to shame the Jews, they being a people of light or knowledgeable of God as opposed to the gentiles who were not, the end result was the same: the gentiles would also be added to God's kingdom.

The great multitude that St. John sees are the gentiles, who like the 144,000 Jews have kept the laws of God and have been cleansed by the blood of Christ. They are now worthy to be with God and serve Him.

They passed the test of the world and proved that they are worthy to be with God by living in the world the way God wanted them to live, with devotion to God love for their fellow man. They passed and survived the many pit falls and traps of the earth and withstood the evil, never losing sight of God, never losing faith that God was always there to help them and that He died for all sins.

Therefore, the two groups are joined together in preparation for entry into heaven. The Jews, because of God's promise to Abraham, are given a special ceremony of being sealed on their foreheads as a sign that God has blessed them as a nation and prepared them through His instruction to receive His son, Jesus, to which the Jews responded well, at least the few who didn't fall away from God. The gentiles, because they adhered to the word of God once they were exposed to that word and lived according to His laws, are also prepared for entry into heaven.

It is evident that at this point, God is readying His people, Jews and non-Jews from every race of the earth, for the glory, which they earned by their good deeds. They are to take their place with Him in His kingdom and never to shed another tear or suffer strife or be subjected to any suffering ever again. The reign of God is at hand. His will has been accomplished.

Chapter 10

The Seventh Seal and the First Six Trumpets

Chapter 8 begins the seventh and final seal, which continues the destruction of earth. Note closely that only a part of the earth will sustain punishment. God, through His means, will cause a nuclear war, which will take place on the third part of the earth and will destroy much, if not all, of it. This is indicated by the first of the seven trumpets: "And the first angel sounded the trumpet, and there followed hail and fire mingled with blood, and it was cast upon the earth; and the third part of the earth was burnt up, and the third part of the trees were burnt up, and all green grass was burnt up."

Upon impact of the nuclear device, the third part of the earth was burnt. God's holocaust is always described by brimstone, pointing clearly that it is man's doing and not God. After the detonation on the land came a detonation on the sea. The sounding of the second trumpet states this: "And the second angel sounded the trumpet, and as it were, a great mountain burning with fire was cast into the sea; and the third part of the sea became blood; and there died the third part of those creatures that have life in the sea, and the third part of the ships was destroyed."

Note that in the last verse, ships were mentioned as an indication that this is a nuclear war. If it were not the fact, ships being destroyed would not have been mentioned. The bombing was strategic. In other words, the third part of the world's navy was destroyed.

The third trumpet tells of the pollution of the nuclear holocaust, which poisons the water of the third part of earth: "And the third angel sounded the trumpet, and there fell from heaven a great star, burning like a torch, and it fell upon the third part of the rivers and upon fountains of water. The name of the star is called Wormwood. And the third part of the water became wormwood; and many people died of the water because they were made bitter."

The third trumpet sequence tells that there may be another detonation on the third part of the world, a nuclear missile, which will poison all the water in that area. This time, the missile is given a name because it will cause the water to become bitter, or wormwood.

The fourth trumpet tells of the death of the third part of the earth by denoting that neither the sun nor the moon nor the stars will shine on the third part of the earth, which is interpreted as atmospheric conditions that will blot out all light from the third part of the earth. This is told in the verse that the third part of them might be darkened and the day for the third part of it might not shine and the night likewise.

This passage means that there will be a haze over the third part of earth that will not let any natural light shine through.

The three woes tell of the impending catastrophes that will plague the earth, her inhabitants, and those living on the third part of earth: "And I beheld, and I heard the voice of an eagle flying in mid-heaven, saying with a loud voice, 'Woe, Woe. Woe, to the inhabitants of earth.'" This was said because of the rest of the trumpeted voices of the three angels, who were about to sound the trumpet.

Chapter 9 begins the sounding of the fifth trumpet, which tells of a great geological disturbance, a great volcanic eruption. Unlike the second trumpet, it shows that this catastrophe is a natural or a God sent event. It is signaled by the passage of a star that fell from heaven, and then given non animated form by denoting that he has the key to the bottomless pit and opened it: "And the fifth angel sounded the trumpet, and I saw that a star had fallen from heaven upon the earth, and there was given to him the key of the bottomless pit. And he opened the bottomless pit, and there came up smoke out of the pit like the smoke of a great furnace; and the sun and the air were darkened by the smoke of the pit."

The particular words, "And he opened the bottomless pit, and there came up smoke out of the pit like the smoke of a great furnace," suggests that the there will be a great volcanic eruption greater than the Mount St. Helens that spewed smoke and ash for hundreds of miles. The whole area was darkened by the mighty volcanic blast that leveled tress and scorched many hundreds of acres of land. The smoke released by the eruption blanketed the area for hundreds of miles and could be seen by the entire area.

On a Public Broadcasting Service (PBS) documentary on volcanic eruption, Mount Vesuvius, was covered. It was the volcano eruption that destroyed Pompeii and Herculaneum. It was found that the inhabitants of Herculaneum were trapped and killed by the volcanic ash from Vesuvius; they did not escape from the eruption as once believed. This was discovered by excavating the site that revealed the bodies all clutched together in a building near their sea resort-like village. They could not out run the rushing smoke and ash and perished while trying to escape to boats on the docks.

The story was a sad story because it told how these people where ancient enterprising people and that the area was really a beautiful resort like city for the wealthy. Many of the buildings were still intact because the lava flow engulfed and preserved them along with the many articles of daily life: tables, pottery, even a bowl of figs and eggs that someone was preparing to eat for breakfast as some might in modern times. All ended by an eruption of Vesuvius.

"And there was given to them power, as the scorpions of the earth have power. And they were told not to hurt the grass of the earth or any green thing or any tree; but only the men who do not have God's seal upon their foreheads. And they were not permitted to kill anyone, but to torture them for five months."

Along with the volcanic eruption, God will send a plague of insects that only have the purpose to inflict pain on men who are not marked by God on their foreheads. It is a sign that God will inflict much suffering, and that will be the beginning of the end. Remember, this will be happening on the third part of the earth where the world is still largely pagan. The catastrophes will be fused with wars, seemingly a limited nuclear war that has also scared that region, but the effect will be far reaching and will affect all of mankind.

In the ensuing Bible passages, the plague is given animation: "And in appearance, the locusts were like horses made ready for battle; and there were on their heads crowns as it were like gold; and their faces were like faces of men. And they had hair like the hair of women; and their teeth were like the teeth of lions. And they had breastplates like breastplates of iron, and the sound or their wings was like the sound of many horses chariots running to battle. And they had tails like those of scorpions and there were stings in their tails; and they had power to harm mankind for five months."

The animation symbolizes the plague that will reach a large area. For this reason, they are like horses. The crown of gold means a wealthy nation was behind it; faces of men suggest it was started for justice's sake; the hair represents strength; the teeth, pain; breast plate, war; the sounding of wings, that it will spread quickly; and the tails also that it will inflict pain and suffering. All of these are symbolic of a plague that is sent after the volcanic eruption. Remember, a number of things will happen one after another: a war will rage in a region of the world; nuclear weapons will be deployed, which means nuclear fallout; and a deadly disease will be rampant causing much suffering.

The only example of how deadly and horrible nuclear devices are was the bombing of Hiroshima, Japan. Through testing, it was found out that the bomb vaporized everything that was in the impact zone. A steel tower used to raise the test bomb was completely gone, vaporized when the bomb was ignited. There was no trace of it. The heat generated by this bomb is extremely intense as the results of the test indicated. When dropped on Hiroshima, people who were caught outside were vaporized—only dark imprints where left on the cement where they were standing as a negative exposure of their once existence.

Soldiers were used as a test to see if an army could withstand the bomb and find out ways to protect soldiers from the deadly weapon in the field. The soldiers were told to dig fox holes and cover themselves with special garments to ward off the heat and deadly rays generated by the nuclear bomb. The soldiers told the frightening story that when the bomb was ignited, they could see their own bones because the x-rays from the blast were so strong. It was very frightening to them.

There is much destruction from nuclear devices. Studies showed that the radiation caused by the bomb at Hiroshima took many lives long after the bomb was deployed. It as revealed that many birth defects were a result of that bomb. It had long-lasting effects even to this day.

The sixth trumpet describes how after a nuclear detonation, mushroom clouds and fallout are evident. Soldiers will pass through the third part of earth and kill the remaining inhabitants or army that resist.

This is stated symbolically in verse 13 of chapter 9: "And the sixth angel sounded the trumpet and I heard a voice from the four horns of the golden altar which is before God, saying to the sixth angel who had the trumpet, 'Loose the four angels who are bound at the great river Euphrates,' and the four angels were loosed who had been kept ready for the hour and day and month and year, that they might kill the third part of mankind. And the number of the army of horsemen was twenty thousand times ten thousand. I heard the number of them."

Therefore, it is evident that many soldiers (two hundred million) will pass through the third part of the earth to subdue the remaining armies. The verse goes on to tell how the soldiers will use conventional methods to defeat the armies of the third part of the world. This is stated symbolically in verse 17-19: "And this is how I saw the horses in the vision; they who sat upon them had breast plates like to fire and to hyacinth and to sulphur, and the heads of the horses were like the heads of lions; and from their mouths issued fire and smoke and sulphur. By these three plagues the third part of mankind was killed, by the fire and the smoke and the sulphur, which issued from their mouth. For the power of the horses is in their mouths and in their tails. For there tails are like serpents, and have heads, and with them they do harm."

The first part of the passage tells that there will be a great army gathered to fight in the third part of the world. Two hundred million men have to be a gathering of all the forces that the Allied commands could muster to defeat a mighty army such as the Orient or China, whose army is the largest in the world. It also suggests that tanks will flow over the third part of earth. This is given in the passage, "And the heads of the horses were like the heads of lions; and from their mouths issued fire and smoke and sulphur," which suggests fiery forces of destruction. God uses brimstone for heavenly fiery destruction. Also, note that the lion symbolizes England. From the number of soldiers that are assembled, it suggests that the Allies are involved in the war. England alone cannot field an army of this magnitude. She is an island nation, relatively small.

CHAPTER 11

THE SMALL SCROLL AND
THE SEVENTH TRUMPET

Chapter 10 states that St. John must go and prophecy again to many nations and peoples and tongues and kings. It also announces that God's mysteries will be accomplished. This means that God has caused many things to happen on earth that have befallen man. God has not shown Himself too many times after the death of Christ. He has not frequented with man as He did with their elders; this was the same for Christ also.

The small scroll contains all the promises that God has made and the many witnesses to His powers, goodness, and fairness. There are three scrolls associated with Revelation. The first has to do with divine providence and is mentioned in the fifth chapter; the last is the scroll of life, which records the deeds of all who have lived on earth and is mentioned in the twenty-first and twenty-second chapters. The small scroll, as stated, contains all of God's promises from the promise to Adam of a savior, to Abraham, to the righteous being with Him in paradise after the Second Coming of Christ as judge of all mankind.

One of the first witnesses to be visited by God other than Adam was Henoch. God said that Henoch was a perfect man and took Henoch to heaven with Him after a completion of a visit with him on earth. "God walked with Henoch, and Henoch was seen no more on earth" (Gn 5:21-23).

It has to be remembered that God created the earth and would come down from heaven to visit the earth. The earth was like a garden and actually was called the garden of pleasure in the book of Genesis. Therefore, God would actually walk on earth as a man would walk in a beautiful garden to relax and be in accord, aesthetically. It was God's creation and it was extremely beautiful, something that was not dead but alive, teeming with life. Life was everywhere, but the supreme creation of God was man. He enjoyed this creature more than any other. Man was a mirror image of God in a contained sense because man was not endowed with supernatural powers.

Henoch was a man whom God intended man to be like. God did not want man to be like the fallen man, Adam. When God saw Henoch and observed his mannerism, righteousness, simplicity, and genuine nature, God took him to heaven with Him. As a reward Henoch was a witness to God. He was the epitome of God's creation, man. God had not failed, His design was not totally flawed.

Although God found a man that He knew was good the way He intended man to be, the majority of men were extremely evil. As the world progressed, this became evident. The condition on earth, the garden of pleasure, had also corrupted angels who were visiting earth masked as men. Contemplating the mental capacity of an angel, one can understand why God became alarmed at angels visiting earth. Even Albert Einstein could not match the mental acuteness of an angel, and probably thousands sowing seeds on earth would cause great alarm in heaven. The offspring of these men were called the mighty men of old as stated in the Bible.

God had created the world so that it would be self-generating, which would have been if held to perfection by God. But God had removed the perfection of the Holy Spirit from the earth and left man on his own. The angelic seed, although mighty, would also produce evil since man had proven to be inclined to evil and would eventually succumb to it. Albert Einstein gave the atomic bomb to our nation. An offspring of an angel would have produced this many years prior to Einstein and many other things one cannot imagine. With that complexity in the world, God decided to destroy it. It was still beautiful, but it was now contaminated and would self-destruct before God could reap a good crop of men to restore earth to its intended sublime splendor.

It saddened God to destroy the world, but He had to rid it of its evil and the angelic seed. He looked around and found Noah, another man whom God knew was good, righteous, simple, and genuine. This man could rejuvenate the earth once God destroyed it and put it back on the path where it was before angels tampered with it. The story continues with Noah being told to build the ark and place all animals in it to save the earth and renew it.

Then, God visited Moses after he had escaped from Egypt and was living abroad. Moses was wanted for killing an Egyptian who was tormenting his countrymen. Although he lived in the Pharaoh's house, free and wealthy, he lamented that his people were captive to the Egyptians.

God had made a promise to the father of Moses's people that their nation would be great, and it was time for that promise to be fulfilled. Moses was chosen by God to deliver his countrymen out of bondage to a place that was chosen and destined for them. This land was told to Abraham, the father of the people that God would save from bondage.

These men were made aware of God's existence because God showed Himself to them. They found favor with God and were pleasing to Him. They became witnesses to heaven. They knew in an instant when God showed Himself that all that was said about heaven was true and there was really a supreme being who created the entire universe. The whole story from the beginning came to life dramatically, vividly, all of the stories of the elders who were true.

As a prophet, St. John became fully aware of God and all of His powers just as the others who had had an experience with God. As the other prophets, he also became fully aware of man just through the comparison between God and man. As St. Augustine puts it: "Man is totally lost, mainly savagely misguided. His life is almost futile with little hope because the way they follow is the way of the world, a path way that will lead them to damnation."

St. John, as other prophets and saints, felt the unfulfillment of life in a spiritual sense and could not adjust totally to man; therefore, they could not adjust after the witness to God, which led many of them to live in barren places. God termed it: "You man, do not deserve their company" (Heb 11:37). This is because they were full of good, righteousness, and honor for both God and man. They really didn't fit in a wicked, sinful world. This also includes some righteous men who didn't actually have an experience with God but had the tremendous faith that God existed and chose to live in accord with God's ideals. Christ calls these men blessed because they had not seen but still believed.

One morning on a TV ministry, a minister came on the air addressing the problems the youth are facing: adjustments, problems, and peer pressures that confront them. He said in so many words once a person joins the world in its thoughts mode and practices its ways, the person can no longer belong to himself. If he departs for the correct paths once again, the world will not trust him; those who are still in the world will deem him a person who had betrayed them.

In pondering the words of the minister, examples of people that actually fall in that category are astounding (many). They were deemed crazy and were not trusted by those who were "in the world." It was all right if one stayed in church and followed its teachings for when one fell, he was gladly welcomed as long as he stayed there. But to return to the church was not acceptable to those who were in the world. The world had no place for them.

It was the shortcomings of man that led many to isolated lives coupled with the fact that they were not accepted by the world. "They are of the world and will not accept you as they did not accept the saints and the prophets who proceeded you" (Mt 23:32-36). But yet they continue to speak the word of God so that others who could see through the darkness could be saved.

Another television minister used St. Paul's writing to distinguish or make a distinction between born-again Christians and those of the world. The gist of his teaching was that the born-again Christian does not think, act, or behave like the world.

When a Christian is born again, he has a different outlook on life, a spiritual outlook in which he does not follow the world. When the world lies, he remains steadfast to truth. When hurt, he forgives as many times as he is hurt. He does not defile his body with drugs, alcohol, and any other foreign substance for the sake of euphoria. He looks weird to the world, but the world respects him because he exemplifies the meek of the earth. He does not upset the world. The world poses no challenge to him. He knows he belongs to God and nothing in the world is that important enough to separate him from God. He also realizes that men of the world can be saved through his good example. Therefore, he does not do as the world does but instead puts on the white robe given by God—the robe the saints wear, the robe of righteousness.

He went on to explain the divisions that the devil creates, namely racism. Everyone knows the hate is generated by this simple division. It seems natural on the surface, but it has deep, evil roots. Men have murdered one another because of misplaced or racial pride that has no place with God because He made man in His image and likeness. He explained that all men have the potential to be saved because Christ died for all men, none excluded. The devil, however, through enmity primarily due to greed causes strife and sin. Blacks were enslaved because of greed or monetary gain, and whites excluded every race to obtain and maintain wealth. The greatness of this minister is heightened, however, when he exclaimed that we as blacks should forgive our white brothers for the atrocities wrought by their ancestors and in turn for whites to right the grievous wrong inflicted by the imposed slavery upon blacks that has deep, ugly scars up to this present time.

Digressing, one could say that men lived alone because they chose to do so. God did not call for it and Christians should be very careful when living isolated in communes. There have been many horrible incidents when the leadership of one goes astray and lead many astray. These men were users of mankind; they were false prophets whom God warned about. Be careful, there are many such men who still exist today.

Proceeding to verse 8, St. John eats the open scroll that was sweet in his mouth but bitter in his stomach. This represents that he will go out and prophesy what he has seen, and the words will be sweet, but no one will heed the words that will make him sick to his stomach. This is given to us in verse 11: "And they said to me, the angels, 'Thou must prophesy again to many nations and peoples and tongues and kings.'"

To see and know that God's kingdom is coming is a beautiful thing and is even sweet to the senses; but, on the other hand, when those good tidings are told to men and they do not heed them, it is a difficult thing because St. John knows that souls will be lost. It gave him a feeling of hopelessness, a forlorn feeling, despair when the sweet words of God falls on deaf ears. It is as if the words of God are in vain.

Many have not adhered to the words of God and have been lost. Revelation is simply a promise that is witnessed by St. John in animation. It tells of the end of man's attempts to deal with both his own inadequacies and Satan. This end will be followed by paradise restored with only those who have proven to be worthy to live in it with God. They have passed through the tribulations and have been washed clean by the blood of Christ. They are from every race and nation, too numerous to count.

Chapter 11 tells how St. John is told to measure the temple of God, the altar, and those who worship therein. Also, God tells St. John that two witnesses will be sent to tell of His kingdom. This is why God wanted St. John to physically measure His temple. In other words, He wanted to let it be known that the temple truly exists, physically.

The two witnesses are the two righteous elders whom God took into heaven, body and soul: Henoch and Elijah. They are called witnesses because they are the only living men besides Christ who were brought to heaven body and soul; they have seen God and have seen heaven. The passage, "These are the two olive trees, and the two lamp stands that stand before the Lord of the earth," means that God came down to earth to be with these men and took them to heaven with Him. They stand with Christ in heaven.

The following passage tells what esteem He has for them, because He gave them power to shut heaven so that it will not rain during the days of their prophesying, which will include prophesying over the waters to turn them into blood and smiting the earth with every plague as often as they desire. If anyone desires to harm the witnesses, "fire will come out of their mouths, and will devour their enemies. And if anyone desires to injure them, he must in this manner be killed."

As a living proof that God and heaven exists, God took Henoch and Elijah with Him into heaven. This bodily extraction from the earth carries two implications with it. First, God promised salvation to men, but men have to abide deeply by God. Meaning, man has to keep all of God's laws before man could be with Him in heaven. These men not only satisfied that requirement, but they surpassed it by being perfect. They not only kept God's laws but they could not conceive of anything else. It was deeply ingrained in their nature.

Simply speaking, many persons must make a totally conscious effort to adhere. With these two men, the effort was totally embedded in their character. Secondly, because of their perfection as an example to the world, they were admitted to heaven body and soul, exonerated from physical death. The only other being to be taken into heaven was God Himself, in the image of Jesus because Jesus is God made man, He is in a class by Himself; but Henoch and Elijah were ordinary men in terms of being conceived through ordinary means as their births were not miraculous as Christ's.

It was included that these men were taken to heaven body and soul without death because they could have been subject to death; but since their perfection had to be recorded, they were spared death. They had lived their lives as Adam should have—without sin, completely obedient to God—and they did not know death as Adam would not had if he had not sinned.

Henoch's and Elijah's being spared death gave God His two witnesses to His powers and also to His promise of both heaven and paradise as He intended for Adam, the first man. They are examples for all mankind and have witnessed God and His powers while on earth and have seen and been in heaven. Who else could be better witnesses to God and for God since they exemplified an extreme dedication to God and His holy will?

In reading the foregoing passages and chapters about how God planned everything for man from the beginning of time when the foundation of earth was laid, one might ask the question, how did all of this get started? Why was the earth made in the first place?

While growing up, I can always remember in my religion classes the answer to that question was God made us to know, love, and serve Him in this world.

This is true because it is stated in the Bible that we must love God with all of our heart and soul and serve Him as our lord and master. But what prompted God to make the universe and the earth? Was it like the poem, "God was lonely so He decided to make a world"?

The answer to the question of why God made the world could be answered in the mirror image of God, which is man. God made us in His image and likeness. Does God get lonely? No! Then why did He make the world, which includes man? The answer could be that it was a creative urge. Remember, we are made in the image and likeness of God. Therefore, if we are creative, then God is creative.

It must have been more than and impulse for God to make the universe and the world because God is not impulsive, we are. But God's mind is much more than ours. Therefore, it may have started with an impulse, then a strong creative desire to create something like Himself, but to a much lesser extent.

Knowing the awesome powers of God, we can visualize how the total creative process went and added from the very beginning. There existed God in a pure supernatural state. Even in this state, there still existed the mirror qualities that both God and man have (tristate quality).

With God, the qualities are much more developed. Basically, His thinking is three dimensional: past, present, and future. Therefore, when God decided to create, He needed to have form as a pattern, or identification, for His creation to attune to. The supernatural God needed no form. The first form that this purely supernatural being took was God the Father. "In the beginning was the Word, and the Word was with God; and the Word was God" (Jn 1:1). From conception of the Creation, the whole of everything was conceived by God: God's form, angels, universe, world, man, and everything else in between each. This was one complete thought by the supernatural God. The word is the culmination because man, the last to be created, has to be saved to be with God once again in the creative plain.

Without form, there could be no angels; they could not know God on God's plain. Therefore, a plain had to be created for them to exist in a communal state with the supernatural God, now God the Father. The same is true for man. "And the Word became flesh and dwelt among us" (Jn 1:14). That being in the Trinity that dwells among us is Christ. We, in our present state cannot be with God. This is the reason why Christ did not want anyone to touch Him because he was going to the Father (Jn 20:17).

All of the above happened as the supernatural God started to create. He knew what was going to take place with every facet, with both heaven and earth, before they were formed. At that point in both creations, heaven and earth, plans were made to effect both in a very, here me, very precise manner, although their creation were millions of earth years apart. This is the quality of God's mind and abilities.

When Christ was born, He became the God being that man could identify with, the being that would rule our plain, so to speak. This is why it is stated in the Bible that Christ has complete dominion over the earth as its sovereign lord. It is an extremely brilliant plan by God to create defined existence, an existence that would never end. Once created, it is never destroyed—God's intent.

Therefore, one can see that the whole of the matter of our being is a creative urge by God. But it is so lofty that I cannot find a word to describe it. It defies our imagination, imagination that is a mirror image of God but could never come close to God's.

Don't let the mission to God be detracted by a definition of the Creation. Our mind will never completely understand God. It was be discussed only to give insight into God, with the intent of bringing one closer to this very awesome being who has the tenderness to love us very dearly as His creation. Nothing else matters but that love He has for us, which should be reciprocated.

Chapter 12

The Story of the Struggle with Satan

Chapter 12 is a summary of the entire struggle with Satan from the beginning. It tells how the Blessed Virgin Mary gave birth to Christ and how the devil tried to kill her and Christ. The events are told out of sequence. First, the Christ child had attempts on His life, and second, even attempts were made at His life before He was born through the seed of Moses, His ancestor. Then it tells how the devil was thrown down to earth because of his aggressions toward God.

The first attempts at the Messiah that pertains to the Blessed Virgin Mary is found in the beginning of Chapter 12: "And a great sign appeared in heaven:" This was the angel announcing the birth of Christ to the wise men and the Christmas star that led them to Christ. "A woman clothed with the sun, and the moon was under her feet, and upon her head a crown of twelve stars." This means that the Blessed Virgin Mary is queen of all earth and of heaven. "And being with child, she cried out in her travail and was in anguish of delivery." Another sign was seen in heaven. This was the Christmas star that led the wise men to Christ and the Blessed Virgin Mary.

"And behold a great red dragon having seven heads and ten horns, and upon his head seven diadems. And his tail was dragging along the third part of the stars of heaven, and he dashed them to the earth." This means that the devil, who was put out of heaven and caused others who were also put out of heaven to go astray, tried to kill the Blessed Virgin Mary's child, Christ. This is seen by the continuing passage: "And the dragon stood before the woman who was about to bring forth, that when she had brought forth he might devour her son. And she brought forth a male child, who is to rule all nations with a rod of iron; and her child was caught up to God and to His throne." This means that Christ accomplished His godly mission and died for mankind and rose on the third day. He is seated at the right hand of God.

If one were to look even closer at the foregoing passage, especially the passage concerning the dragon, "And behold a great red dragon having seven heads and ten horns, and upon his head seven diadems," one sees that the dragon is animated in symbolist form to display the seven great nations that must come up before the end of the worldly system.

These seven nations are milestones for the time frame of elapsing time before the end. Seven, as stated, denotes an earthy godly perfection. Everything that has to do with earth, in God's plans, has seven for a number in honor of the length of time it took God to make earth. This is why the devil is displayed as a dragon with seven heads and ten horns with seven diadems on its seven heads.

The seven nations are all the great conquering nations starting with Egypt. Although there may be several leaders of the nations, the nations are counted instead of the leaders. The beast coming out of the sea will be covered in chapter 13. All of these nations will be blasphemous to God, meaning they are pagans in nature, except for England and the United States, which are among the nations.

As a prelude to the thirteenth chapter, the beast of that chapter is similar to this beast. The only difference is that, that beast has ten diadems resting on ten horns, whereas this beast has seven diadems resting on the seven heads. The distinction is that the seven diadems symbolize the distinct seven nations and are emphasized by that fact. The horns are leaders as discussed in earlier chapters.

Therefore, we can see that the devil is displayed as a red dragon because the nations that are depicted are not godly nations and most are pagan in nature. Although the United States and England are two of these nations whose basic make up is Christian in nature, they are part of an earthly system imperfect with its citizenship in sin, therefore, blasphemous to God.

Being out of sequence with the world events, chapter 12 starts off with Christ and the Blessed Virgin Mary. The Blessed Virgin Mary fled with Christ and hid until it was safe for her and Christ once again. This is shown by the continuing passage: "And the woman fled into the wilderness, where she has a place prepared by God, that there they may nourish her a thousand two hundred and sixty days."

The Christian story is a very familiar story that is known throughout the world. Here, the story is told briefly but all the particulars are given. The great sign in heaven is the Christmas star that led the wise men to the Christ child. How Mary was chosen by God to bring Christ into the world is told by the description of the woman: "She being clothed with the sun and the moon being under her feet with twelve stars as a crown upon her head." All of this tells of the special favor bestowed upon her.

For those who do not have closed minds, from my description of events and general things in this book, you should be able to see that I have in actuality touched base with God. Here I want to introduce you the very holy and supreme woman, Mary. Mary was a very young maiden when God sent the angel Gabriel to announce His will for her. She was very frightened and totally confused by the appearance of Gabriel. Remember, angels are very captivating beings, they are very beautiful and flawless in features.

With the above, I would like to describe the Blessed Virgin Mary to you. She, as I said, was a young maiden but very beautiful. She looked like both an Israeli and an Arab girl, very beautiful. She has very dark eyes and a light brown complexion, like an Israeli girl. Her hair is dark, as an Israeli or an Arab girl's would be. If she were to walk in any mall in the United States or abroad, she would be stared at by many and strongly glanced at by others. She is that beautiful, but more so in her heavenly state. I have never seen the tomb of Bernadette, only a glimpse on TV, but she strongly resembles the picture I saw of Bernadette, whom the Blessed Virgin Mary appeared to in Lourdes, France.

The Virgin Mary was not the only divine being that appeared to me when I was a child. The holy family appeared to me while I sat on my grandmother's front porch. I will not give a full description of the child Jesus, except that He was handsome, with curly hair. In the appearance, the Christ child bore the complexion of all races. This was a message to me. It is hard to explain, but His complexion was a dark brown, even more so than the Virgin Mary.

St. Joseph was young and handsome. I could see the strength of moral character in his face. From that, I understood why God had chosen him for the foster father role. At the time of the appearance, I didn't understand why they appeared to me and thought it was a hoax being played on me by my older cousin Joe by shining a camera in the sky. Later, when Christ came back to help me in my life's journey, I understood the appearance in its entirety.

I told no one of the appearance, but one day while looking at a stature of Mary, it brought back the appearance, and I decided to tell my third-grade class of the appearance of Mary. Mary is so beautiful that I always carried her in my heart in a special way, the reason I forgot about Christ and St. Joseph, telling only of her. Later, when Christ came back to help me, He made me realize that He was paramount, He is God.

Since I have seen much of heaven, I thought that I would add this to my book. Not for my glory, but for those who have a very profound, never ending love for Mary. She truly, deeply loves mankind and does everything to help with the bringing of mankind to salvation. I wager that to this day she is still asking Christ to do miracles for those who are in need, just as the wine she asked her son, Christ, to materialize at the wedding feast. Who could refuse a loving, beautiful woman, a woman who nurtured and protected Him (Christ) while on earth?

In the above main event, it is also told how Mary and Joseph fled from Bethlehem to Egypt to save Christ. The exact word, however, is wilderness. But to God, Egypt is considered a wilderness because it was pagan, therefore spiritually barren.

With that journey to Egypt, Christ was saved from the devil, the red dragon as depicted here who is really guised as Herod, the tyrant ruler who ordered that every child aged two years and younger be killed in an effort to kill Christ, whom he thought would be king over his realm.

It was told by the prophets of old that the Jews would have a messiah that would save them. This prophecy was announced many times by the prophets; therefore, the Jews awaited this event and even looked forward to it immensely.

This story of the Messiah was also told to the countries around Israel since they knew of them, and possibly their scholars had recorded the deeds of the Israelites and the help of their God. Hence, this story created much concern for those who had conquered the Jews when it was heard that it was about time the Messiah would be born as the scriptures said.

Herod was afraid that this Jewish king would take his throne from him; therefore, he ordered that every male child approximately Christ's age be killed when he learned from the Magi that Christ had actually been born in Bethlehem (Mt 2:5).

The Magi, three traveling kings, had stopped in his country to rest. Upon visiting Herod, they told him of the king who had been born and to whom they were seeking to pay homage because they had seen his sign in the heavens (Mt 2:2). This is the great sign that is mentioned in chapter 12:1 of Revelation. It was this same star that led the Magi to Christ after their meeting with Herod.

In telling this phase of the story of the struggle with Satan, his attempts at ending God's promise of salvation, one can see how the Bible uses its symbol structure to isolate the main milestones of salvation, one being the birth of Christ. This phase is set off by the symbol of "a great sign seen in Heaven," which was told in the Bible that a great star appeared to the Magi, the three kings, announcing the birth of Christ. This symbol sets apart another story of the beginning of the Jewish nation, or Israel. At that point, the symbol was a river. This suggests that the two main parts are divided and distinct: the story of Moses, the second milestone, being saved by a river and the story of Christ's birth announced dramatically by the giant star. The sequence is out of order because the Christ child's story is told first and Moses being told second with the story of Satan, who started the struggle in the middle, being cast out of heaven.

The correct order of the events should be, of course, Satan cast out of heaven, then the story of Moses, and last the word made flesh: the salvation threshold, birth, life, and death of Christ and salvation gained by His death and resurrection.

These events in chapter 12 of Revelation are, in reality, the story of God and His divine lordship over all and are the main events that concern salvation. Since it is the entire struggle with the devil, it is told in chapter 12, twelve being a heavenly perfect number and symbolizing God the Father's domain or jurisdiction. It is a complete story in itself with everything escalating from paradise lost by Adam.

Even before Adam, it tells of the loss of heaven by Lucifer, the devil, who exercises his powers of destruction because of this loss of heaven. He and his followers participated in their continuous struggle with good even after the birth of Christ. This seemingly never-ending struggle raging between good and evil will last until God calls a halt to everything and claim the good for Himself. Then paradise will start over once again. Men should, by that time, have learned that it is God who makes things perfect, not man. With that, man could live in peace, abiding by God without the devil's temptation abounding.

As stated, the sequence of events is not in the order of occurrence. In verse 7 of chapter 12, it is told that the mighty angel Michael battled with the devil and throws him to earth. This is seen in the passage: "And there was a battle in heaven: Michael and his angels battled with the dragon, and the dragon fought and his angels. And they did not prevail, neither was their place found any more in heaven. And that great dragon was cast down, the ancient serpent, he who is called the devil and Satan, who leads astray the whole world, and he was cast down to the earth and with him his angels were cast down."

God had made heaven and the angels. Of the angels, God created one that was the most beautiful of all, one whom He loved dearly, Lucifer. It was said that Lucifer had more power than any of the others. And it was that God-given gift that led him to his destruction.

Lucifer, because he had immense powers, thought that he could rule heaven; therefore, he denounced God and gathered a following in an attempt to overthrow God, which was very fatal to him because God's legions of angels threw Lucifer and his followers out of heaven. Although God defeated Lucifer, he retained all of the powers endowed to him by God. This is what makes him so diabolical. He has a tremendous mental capacity not equaled by the majority of angels, mental capacity not as we know it in terms of human mental capacity, but in terms of that which is far superior to human beings. This is why God says that even the elect purify themselves when Satan is loosed (Jb 41:16). It signifies that Lucifer is very powerful.

Lucifer lost heaven, and his hatred toward God still persists. This is the reason that he leads man astray because he knows that God loves man. This outlook is the same as that of evil men: if they cannot hurt you, they hurt something near you in an effort to revenge themselves, knowing it will hurt you. Lucifer is a master at leading man away from God. He does everything he can to achieve this, knowing he has nothing to lose because he has lost.

Man, just as the angels, has a free will, but he also has an innate sense of right and wrong. Since he is a created being, he is not destroyed but is granted an eternal existence; thus, he must be confined or, in a fine sense, contained and defined by God. This is the reason for hell that Christ speaks of (Mt 5:29-30). All beings must be constrained either in a good place, a place of proof, or a place of purification. If the sins are irremovable and unrepented, then the purification is eternal. Thus, we have the never-ending fires of hell.

Satan knows this and will stop at nothing to keep man away from God by his devious means. He also knows his time is short; therefore, with haste he manipulates his war using every trick in his repertoire. The closer a person is to God, the more he works at that person because the gratification is intensified when that person falls.

The following passage tells how heaven rejoiced when the devil and his followers were cast down to earth. Briefly, it tells that they also rejoiced when the inhabitants of earth, who were Christians and kept Gods word, overcame the devil through the blood of Christ. The Christians are the martyrs who worked and died for Christ, bore witness to Christ, and died for that witnessing. The heavens will also mourn for the earth and the sea because the devil will catch many of the earth's inhabitants in his fury since he knows he has a short time to live.

"And I heard a loud voice in heaven saying, 'Now has come the salvation, and the power and the kingdom of our God, and the authority of his Christ, for the accuser of our brethren has been cast down, he who accused them before our God day and night. And they overcame him through the blood of the Lamb and through the word of their witness, for they did not love their lives even in face of death. Therefore, rejoice, O heavens, and you who dwell there in. Woe to the earth and to the sea because the devil has gone down to you in great wrath, knowing that he has but a short time.'"

If one keeps an open mind, a segment of the Quran reveals a possible cause of the struggle with Satan or possibly a tool he used to gather forces for his attempts at the throne of God.

The Quran expressed an idea that the angels in heaven were not pleased with God's placing man, His creation, in a garden of pleasure as even the Bible described it, before the angels. Man was a newcomer and didn't seem worthy by the angels' standards to receive so noble a gift, especially after the angels saw what the pleasures were.

One could ponder, how could angels be jealous of any human state when it is so limited, and an angel's power is so much more astounding than man's? One must remember that man was truly innocent with the Holy Spirit keeping everything in balance. He was not, as men are now, subjected to everything that can be imagined. Rather, man was tended. He had no cravings. Habits would not stay with him; the Holy Spirit took these away from him because he was pure and innocent.

It is the habitual element in man that causes a difficult road for him once he strays from the purity of, let's say, mind and body. Without his aid from the Holy Spirit, man craves for things that heighten his senses. It is this craving or habit that leads man further away from God because it becomes a weakness of the flesh, things that man has to control on his own since the Holy Spirit does not tend man as he did in the beginning. Many sins fall in this category, habitual because many do become habitual. Things such as lying, stealing, lust, etc.

To compensate for this flaw in man, fasting was instituted. Fasting in itself strengthens the body and the mind because it builds a will. Through that will to deny oneself of basal needs as food, which most fasting is for, other things habitual can be refused. Thus, the urge for the sensation is diminished and resolved.

Normally, in a matter of a week or two, depending on the type of habit or what is being misused. Because a habit could be broken just as fast as it takes to begin it. For example, smoking cigarettes, which is a hard habit to break if you have ever been hooked on them, is a habit that is broken in a matter of weeks with concentration. The urge leaves. One abstains from cigarettes, but even one backslide can rekindle the urge and put him back on the cigarette habit once again.

Cigarette smoking is an example to illustrate or animate the topic discussed, not to criticize it as an evil of life, although for many it well might be (not to term it sinful).

It was probably before Adam and Eve's sin that caused the rattling of the angels because this was the heightened existence of man. He was in his purest form then, with no flaws as the angels are. But unlike the angels, he was in a place of sensual pleasure: taste, smell, touch, etc. These senses were probably new to angels and envied by many, which was probably heightened by Satan.

I'll give you an example of how sensual the world is, through a vivid experience I had. As a child, while playing a game with my baby sister, I almost suffocated. When the air returned though my nostrils again, it was literally sweet as honey. I shall never forget that sensation. We take many of earth's pleasures in the form of taste, smell, and touch for granted.

In Genesis 6:2-7, God destroyed the world because of the misuse of the human gift of life. Man was very wicked and evil. Even the angels joined, taking human form to be with women; it was too much for God. Therefore, He destroyed the earth in grief and rejuvenated it with Noah's seed. Mankind became extremely evil with evil in their hearts at all times. Noah would give earth a fresh start.

Hence, we have a phrase in the Bible, "For the accuser of our brethren has been cast down, he who accuse them before God day and night. And they overcame him through the blood of the Lamb and through the word of their witness" (Rv 12:10-11). This implies that there is some jealousy behind the accusations made about man stemming from the deemed favoritism toward man by God.

We do not know exactly what caused the struggle between God and Satan. We know that Satan had to become extremely vain and self-centered to challenge God, his creator. The only evidence that we have is a written passage in the

Quran; and keeping an open mind about Ishmael as a loved son of God through Abraham, the account may be valid. The two stories coincide with one another and do somewhat complement each other, thereby strongly suggesting that the ambition of Satan was kindled by God's favoring man and placing him in paradise, or he used it as a rebelling point.

Of course, God's reply to this, the question why man is favored, is that He measures out what He wants to measure out, with no one to rebut Him for it. He is supreme to all, and no one has the authority to question him, let alone challenge him. This is recorded in the parable of the field workers, whom the farmer pays the same wage, although they started work at different times (Mt 20:2-15), and other parables and passages in the Bible.

Passage 13: "And when the dragon saw that he was cast down to the earth, he pursued the woman who had brought forth the male child. And there were given to the woman the two wings of the great eagle, that she might fly into the wilderness unto her place, where she is nourished for a time and times and half time, away from the serpent." This means that the devil tried to kill the Blessed Virgin Mary, but she escaped.

"And the serpent cast out of his mouth after the (woman) water like a river, that might cause her to be carried away by the river." That means that the devil tried to kill Christ's ancestor, here Moses. Moses was placed in a basket and set on the river so he might not be killed, and he was saved. This is shown in the following passage. "And the earth helped the woman, and the earth opened her mouth and swallowed up the river that the dragon had cast out of his mouth:"

The following passage tells how the devil missed Christ and His ancestor, so he went after the inhabitants of earth to lead them astray. This is shown in passage 17: "And the dragon was angered at the woman, and went away to wage war with the rest of her offspring, who keep the commandments of God and hold fast the testimony of Jesus. And he stood upon the sand of the sea." This means he led many astray in his wrath, sand meaning many.

The foregoing passage tells about Moses and how he was saved from being murdered by Pharaoh. It is out of sequence when taken in conjunction with the whole story (world events), yet it is a very important story because through Moses, not only were the Jews saved, but God showed Himself to man announcing that the Israelites were a holy nation belonging to him.

Through that ordeal, God would instruct a nation of people, and salvation will start to take shape. Then came the passing of God's laws, the Ten Commandments, to Moses. This was the start of salvation, but heaven was still closed and would not be open until the death and resurrection of Christ.

It took many years and preparation for the coming of Christ. After He came, He furthered the teachings of the prophets who preceded Him, giving man a very clear understanding of what God the Father wants us to do to be reconciled with Him.

Moses was a key to this story and a milestone. He set the stage for Christ. Christ could have been born at any time, even under bondage with the Israelites during Moses's time; but God's plan was to send His word and laws first by His messenger, the prophets who are His witnesses, then send His only son, Jesus, as a culminating effort to secure man for God. And with Christ's bloodshed, man is saved.

CHAPTER 13

THE BEAST OF THE SEA AND
THE BEAST OF THE EARTH

In chapter 13, St. John tells how he sees a beast coming out of the sea, which will be the Unites States. This is known because it is described as a "leopard, and its feet were like the feet of a bear, and its mouth like the mouth of a lion." This description of the Unites States in Daniel's vision of the first three beasts, the last beast, which is the United States, was left out. The leopard means justice. The United States was born for justice. This is why she split with England. The bear's feet mean that like Japan, it has become powerful and wants to be all noteworthy, and the mouth of a lion means that she is boasting much of her might.

The passage, "having seven heads," means that there will be seven mighty nations of earth, with the seventh being the last before the end. The "ten horns and upon them rest ten diadems, and upon it heads blasphemous names," means that all seven nations had blasphemed before God, even the United States, which is the last.

Further in the passage, one will note that "one head is smitten off, as it were to death: but its deadly wound was healed," which means that England was not dethroned when the United States won her freedom. Remember, the other nations went under, but not England, who is still considered a mighty nation. You will note that the United States is worshipped because she won a major victory over the third part of the earth. This is revealed in the passage "Who is like the beast, and who will be able to fight with it?"

As stated earlier, everything is symbolic and not really dramatically obvious. With that in mind, look at verse 6-10. "And it opened its mouth for blasphemies against God, to blaspheme His name and His tabernacle, and those who dwell in heaven. And it was allowed to wage war with the saints and to overcome them. And there was given to it authority over every tribe, and people, and tongue, and nation. And all the inhabitants of the earth will worship it whose names have not been written in the book of life of the Lamb who has been slain from the foundation of the world. If any man has an ear, let him hear. He who is for captivity, into captivity he goes; he who kills by the sword, by the sword must he be killed. Here is the patience and the faith of the saints."

God the Father promised man that He will avenge all on earth and bids mankind not to be drawn to revenge because it cripples the soul and causes it to be lost. God knows the human psychic and knows that man has tendencies to be very vindictive. He warns that this is not an attribute of a true son of God and promises that all will be avenged no matter what it is. It is weighted and will be returned in kind "Vengeance is mine; I will repay, says the Lord" (Rom 12:19), meaning what ever is done to you will be repaid in equal terms; therefore, don't be dismayed. Christ, during His ministry, said not to give in to evil, but rather do good to defeat it (Mt 5:38).

The above verses state that there will come a time when the United States will blaspheme God's name and His tabernacle and wage war with the saints to overcome them. As stated, these things may not be obvious. It may be over issues or even Christianity's place in our society or both. One example is prayer in the school, the extent of the role it plays, whatever; the beast will win. The key to verses 1-10 in chapter 13 lies in the last passage: "He who is for captivity, into captivity he goes; he who kills by the sword, by the sword must be killed. Here is the patience and the faith of the saints."

St. John sees another beast, but this time it is coming up out of the earth. "And it had two horns like to those of a lamb, but it spoke as does a dragon." This beast is a false prophet. This is known because it had two horns like the lamb, which is Christ, but it goes on to say, "but it spoke as does a dragon," meaning it spoke like the devil, letting St. John know that this beast was guised as a Christ follower, but really the devil, thus false prophet. This beast will make the people on earth worship the first beast. It will work great signs. One is it will make fire come down from heaven upon the earth in the sight of mankind to lead them astray.

The beast will cause all the people of earth, "the small and the great, the rich and the poor, and free and the bond, to have a mark on their right hand or on their foreheads, and it will bring it about that no one may be able to buy or sell, except him who has the mark, either the name of the beast or the number of its name . . . Here is wisdom. He who has understanding, let him calculate the number of the beast, for it is the number of man; and its number is six hundred and sixty six (666)."

Before discussing the numbering system or the number 666, take a look at how crafty the devil is. The mark of the beast is on the right hand and also the forehead, which is the same place (forehead) where God marks His saints. It is an attempt by Satan to confuse the elect of God by emulating the place of the mark.

In the end, many will be led astray. Only the ones who really follow God carefully will be saved. The righteous of God will not be led astray by Satan and will stand steadfast to God's way. At this time, it will be dangerous to join cults as many have done. It is documented what happened to many who joined such cults such as Jim John and David Carish. Here man is following man, not following the word of God. Man should not take part in anything that is not godly in action, word, or deed. That should be the order for all. Don't judge, for you will be judged. Don't condemn, for you will be condemned. Be free from all worldly ideas and be close to God.

To get back to the numbering system, the number 666 is a highly imperfect number since the Trinity is perfect, or the number 3. The number 666 is a remuneration of the number 3, three times. In others words, 6 is repeated three times, a 6 for each person of the Trinity. This denotes that the number is highly imperfect. If the Trinity is perfection, then the opposite of the Trinity is imperfection.

The number 6 is the number of the days it took God to make man. Man was made on day number 6, and he is extremely imperfect. In fact, every thing that

God made works fine: the seasons change, the animals migrate on time, rivers flow to seas, and the planets orbit the sun without mishaps. Everything works just fine except man. He is the only flaw of nature, and this is because he is not tended by the Holy Spirit. He is outside of God and terribly flawed. Therefore, the number 666 is given to him, the mark of man, created on the sixth day and outside the domain of God.

The number on the right hand may signify credit cards or similar devices to recognize an individual, or social security numbers. These cards are held on the right hand since most humans are right handed. Of course, these cards are part of a vast computer system where just about everyone is accounted for like the Social Security system. This is true for the United States, but the same type of systems are in place in many other nations also. This maybe the mark of the beast with which everyone is marked because everyone has such cards.

The devil knows his time is short, therefore, he will pull out every trick he can to lead man away from God. At this stage, he uses a simulation of God. He marks man with a mark on his right hand, which may be an actual mark but could well be a symbolic mark of a numbering system where everyone uses the number with their right hand. The simulated mark on the forehead is confusing because this is the place where God marks the saints of the earth with His name.

Throughout man's history on earth, it has been recorded that the elect of God was shown by the glory of God around their head, or halos that cannot be duplicated by Satan. The mark of God's name on the forehead will clearly distinguish His elect since Satan will use the same means as trickery at the end. God in the end will allow Satan to do so because Satan cannot duplicate anything that God does. But at the end, Satan will come up with his own schemes, which God will allow.

It is very important that the people who dwell on earth at that time know God and His will for mankind. They must stay righteous at all times. Basically, they must do the right things, the things that God wants man to do: stay innocent as children, humble, and kind until the end. When you are caring and loving in all things and all situations, you know that you are doing what God wants you to do and what God wants you to be. In that vein, you cannot be lost to the other side.

CHAPTER 14

THE PROMISE OF SALVATION

In chapter 14, St. John tells of the 144,000 that God will chose, His own from Israel. These are the descendants of Abraham, who are with out blemish. In this chapter, they were singing a chant that only they could learn. God's voice was in the voice of many waters meaning that the earth will be destroyed shortly, or rather, man's system will be destroyed and replaced by God's perfect system.

Looking closer at that passage, passages 2 and 3—"And I heard a voice from heaven like a voice of many waters, and like a voice of loud thunder and the voice that I heard was as of harpers playing on their harps"—one understands that unlike the voice of many waters in earlier chapters, something else was added, that being the harp like quality of the voice.

This quality is added to God's voice because His voice here is a complete story. The quality of the sound of many waters is the upcoming destruction; the quality of thunder, forcefulness; and the last, the quality of harps, that the end has come and now there is peace in a godly system, with the old system being completely destroyed.

In interpreting the Bible, close attention must be made to all changing symbols as they are the key to the intention of the passage, or they fully explain the intent once they are taken in conjunction with the entirety. By adding the two together, one gains insight into the new symbol and can reach a conclusion—in this passage, destruction (voice of many waters), forcefulness (thunder), and peace and harmony (harpers playing their harps).

In continuing verses, St. John tells how an angel preached to the inhabitants of earth to fear God and give Him honor, for the judgments have come. Another claims that Babylon has fallen. Remember, Adam ate of the forbidden fruit of knowledge; well, Babylon, to a higher extent, is that same knowledge. It does not mean Babylon but rather all knowledge that has been accumulated since that time. God was the only source that we needed, and He will be the only source in the new kingdom. Also, Babylon was a pagan kingdom, blasphemous in God's eyes.

The last angel followed saying with a loud voice, "If anyone worships the beast and its image and receives a mark upon his forehead or upon his hand, he also will drink of the wine of the wrath of God, which is poured unmixed into the cups of His wrath; and he shall be tormented with fire and brimstone in the sight of the holy angels and in the sight of the Lamb. And the smoke of their torments goes up forever and ever."

It is very important for Christians to understand that at the end, many will be deceived, the great and the small. Revelation 13:15-16 states this will happen because basically man does not know God, although he thinks he does. We sometimes miss the basic goodness of God and are led in some other direction, thinking that it is God who wants us there. This was the case with Jim Jones and his group or in recent times David Carish.

In the time of the end, there will be many false prophets working signs, fooling the people of earth into believing and worshiping them. This happens because man, as stated, does not know God. He looks to many things, things that he wants to see or believe because it favors his fancy. God has given us the signs to look for in him. A manifestation of the prophets and Christ with all of the brotherly love and understanding that we could give are all the signs needed!

If the people with Jim Jones saw that God is not a separatist, then they could have seen Jim Jones for what he was: just a man who was lost. God does not preach separation, especially when He knows that the world is full of good. God preaches love of neighbor no matter what, not isolation from neighbor because he is wicked. God knows, as Paul preached, the life of a good man is the benefit to all. His is an example, which cannot be denied, and many know he is good and try to fellow in his ways. This is the duty of Christians; they are called by Christ to be that example so others can be saved. "Father I pray that you protect them in the world" (Jn 17:15).

The Bible teaches us to display good Christian examples so that others might see their erring ways and be saved (Mt. 5:16). As a Christian, the love of God should be so strong that it transcends all evil that is around a man and does not lead him to destruction. This is why men are instructed in the ways of God as Christians. The laws are explicit and simple: honor God and God alone, and love thy fellow man as one loves himself.

The Bible prophesied, however, that man will be led astray by signs of wonders. He will hardly ask if it is from God, knowing that the devil has great powers also, but will often follow the workers of the signs and be lost for an eternity. All prophecies from God come to pass or become a reality.

To confuse man further, those who follow the beast will receive a mark either on the forehead or the right hand. It is also known that the chosen of God will receive a mark on their foreheads. The two could be confusing because many won't know which is which, especially when the mark is on the forehead.

Well, just as Christ, Christians will know that God's mark will be on the people who are God fearing and just, righteous to fellow man, good Christians, kind, not overbearing, with love of God in their hearts and love of their fellow man. Christians are hard to separate from the ways of God. It is hard to make them lie or cheat on or even talk about their fellow man. These are the people who have the mark of God on their foreheads and are easily distinguished from the fallen ones who have the mark of the beast on their foreheads and the other distinguishing mark on their right hand.

Basically, God is for good. The devil is not, he is only for worldly things, knowing those are the things with which he can trap mankind. Beware of the workers of great signs. Pray to God for discernment, and study or observe the worker of great signs closely; watch the fruits that they bear. This is an indication of his inner being. Learn the teachings of the prophets and Jesus. Question them thoroughly before you leap. Remember, only God is worshiped. But above all, know God. Christ said, "I know mine, and they know me" (Jn 10:14).

At the end of chapter 14, St. John sees a vision of Christ sitting on a white cloud, and He had a crown of gold and a sharp sickle. He also saw an angel coming out of the temple of heaven with a sharp sickle. The angel told Christ to put forth the sickle and reap because the harvest of the earth is ripe. Christ then released His sickle upon the earth, and the earth is reaped.

Another angel, who had authority over the fire, came from the temple and he called with a loud voice to the angel who had a sickle to put forth his sickle and "gather clusters of the vine of the earth: for its grapes are fully ripe." And the angel cast his sickle and gathered the vintage of the earth and cast it into the great winepress of the wrath of God.

While on earth, Christ gave us the parable of the harvest, where all will be gathered at once. Then the weeds and grass will be separated from the fruit of the harvest and will be caste into the never-ending fires (Mt 13:39-43).

The foregoing passage is telling that the parable, a lesson Christ taught, is in reality about to take place. All through the existence of man, the good have been mixed with the bad, with the good enduring much suffering at the hands of the bad. Many were tormented unbearably by the wicked. Now it is time for the two to be separated. The judgment has come.

The passage tells that the destruction of earth by God is beginning. God the Father is supreme over all of heaven. This is evident because an angel follows Christ out of heaven and delivers the message for Him to cast His sickle upon the earth. Since the angel was coming out of the temple in heaven, we know that God sent him to signal Christ to start the beginning of the judgment.

At this point, the total plan of God for mankind is culminating. He has put into place a culture for man to grow in wisdom and beauty through the arts. Man now has enough knowledge for Christ to be sent, and a complete record of Him could be established for all.

The beginning of the church was started with the Jewish nation; they were given the law to live by and the recognition that God is real and truly exists. They saw many great and wonderful signs to add to their stories of the one true God. The prophets were sent as a constant sign that God was still with the Jewish nation and for them to obey the covenant that was made between God and the Jewish nation.

With their heightened intelligence, Christ came to teach mankind through the Jewish nation. Man had to know what was expected of him in order for him to be with God, in God's new kingdom, His new paradise. Disciples were taught by Jesus Christ Himself to continue His teachings so that all mankind would hear the good news or Gospel of Christ so that they could be saved. The darkness about God was lifted by all the proceeding efforts; now man is given light so that he may understand God's will for him and, especially, that there is truly a living God who created all of this, the world. And that He loves us dearly, but we must abide by Him to be with Him; there is no other way.

CHAPTER 15

THE SEVEN LAST PLAGUES

In chapter 15, St. John tells how he sees the seven angels who hold the seven last plagues for the inhabitants of earth. He also sees those who have overcome the plagues, those who heeded God's words and kept His commandments, standing in the sea of glass. This symbolizes that God will spare them from His eternal wrath as He spared Noah and his children from the waters that He used to destroy the earth. This also symbolizes the waters that He parted for Moses to save the children of Israel from Pharaoh's army. But mainly, the sea of glass is symbolic of the earth's destruction by water.

After seeing those who have overcome, St. John sees the temple of the tabernacle of the testimony was opened in heaven, and there came forth out of the temple the seven angels who had the seven plagues. These angels were clothed in clean white linen, and girt about their breast with golden girdles. This symbolizes that this is the beginning of the judgment.

When God first appeared to St. John, God was dressed in the same manner, but only the color of the garment was not mentioned. His feet were brass to indicate that the signs that He would give St. John are the beginning of the end. His feet glowing like a furnace signify the refining of souls as a furnace refines metal. Also, the brass feet are as the brass sockets in the hanging of the tabernacle or the threshold of the tabernacle, thus a symbol meaning the thresh hold of eternal salvation if God's commandments were kept.

St. John went on to note that one of the four living creatures gave to the seven angels, seven golden bowls full of the wrath of God, who lives forever and ever, and that no one could enter the temple until the plagues of the seven angels were finished.

Chapter 16 tells of the seven plagues the angels pour on the earth.

> And I heard a loud voice from the temple saying to the seven angels, "Go and pour out the seven bowls of the wrath of God upon the earth."
>
> And the first went and poured out his bowl upon the earth, and a sore and grievous wound was made upon the men who have the mark of the beast, and upon those who worshiped its image.
>
> And the second poured out his bowl upon the sea, and it became blood as of a dead man; and every living thing in the sea died. And the third poured out his bowl upon the rivers and fountains of waters, and they became blood. And I heard the angel of the water saying, "thou art just, O Lord, who art and who wast, O Holy One, because thou hast judge these things; because they poured out the blood of saints and prophets, blood also thou hast given them to drink; they deserve it!"
>
> And I heard the altar saying "Yes, O Lord God almighty, true and just are thy judgments."

The second three bowls tell of more for the inhabitants of earth. "And the fourth poured out his bowl upon the sun, and he was allowed to scorch mankind with fire, and mankind were scorched with great heat, and they blasphemed the name of God who has authority over theses plagues, and they did not repent of their works. And the sixth poured out his bowl upon the great river Euphrates, and dried up its water, that a way might be made ready for the kings from the rising sun."

These plagues are not symbolic. These are the actual plight of man before the end.

St. John goes on to tell of the unclean spirits that will try to assemble men to fight against God and His upcoming ending wrath. St. John says the unclean spirit came from the mouth of the dragon, and the beast and false prophets were like frogs. This means that the frogs were spirits of demons working signs and they go forth unto the kings of the whole earth to gather them together for the battle on the great day of God Almighty.

The symbol, frog, was used much earlier in the Bible. It was used in the book of Moses. God sent Moses to Pharaoh announcing that the Jews must be released. And as the story goes, Pharaoh refused. To show Pharaoh that God had sent him, Moses began to work great miracles, which Pharaoh's sorcerers imitated. The last miracle imitated was the miracle of frogs.

Throughout the Bible frogs are symbolic of false prophets. It is done to symbolize that at the end, false prophets will reign no more and also show that their powers fall vastly short of God's.

> And the seventh poured out his bowl upon the air, and there came forth a loud voice out of the temple from the throne, saying, "It has come to pass." And there were flashes of lightning, rumblings and peals of thunder, and there was a great earthquake such as never has been since men were first upon the earth, so great an earthquake was it . . . And the great city came into three parts; and the cities of nations fell. And Babylon the great was remembered. And every island fled away, and the mountains could not be found. And great hail, heavy as a talent came down from heaven upon man; and men blasphemed God because of the plague of the hail; for it was very great.

Chapter 16

The Woman and the Scarlet Beast

In chapter 17, one of the seven angels came to show St. John the woman on the scarlet beast, which is symbolic of Babylon. The whole passage is symbolic of a woman because men loved her and nursed her and also her offspring. Theses, as stated earlier, means knowledge and sin. She was so sinful that she killed anyone who told her to repent of her ways. As passage six stated, "And I saw the woman drunk with the blood of the saints and with the blood of the martyrs of Jesus."

St. John was once again baffled by the symbolism. The angel explained in passage eight.

> The beast that thou sawest was, and is not, and is about to come up from the abyss, and will go to destruction. And the inhabitants of the earth whose names have not been written in the book of life from the foundation of the world will wonder when they see the beast which was, and is not.
>
> And here is the meaning for him who has wisdom. The seven heads are seven mountains upon which the woman sits; and they are seven kings; five of them have fallen, one is, and the other has yet to come;

and when he comes, he must remain a short time. And the beast that was, and is not, is more over himself eight, and is of the seven, and is on his way to destruction.

The seven heads are seven kingdoms that rose up into great power. The Babylonians, the Egyptians, the Greeks, the Romans, and the English are five that fell. The United States is one that will. There will come one after the United States for only a short time, but will go into destruction. England is mentioned as being the one that was and is not. These seven kingdoms all became great; but because of their great sins against God, they fell by the way side. They all drank lavishly of the wine of fornication with the wayward woman.

It is interesting to note, however, that England's ideals and government is very often humane that she seeks to help others that are less fortunate. Often the ideals of the United States, whose birth came out of England, are even higher. The United States is the only other country that has such a just government in terms of humanity for the poor of all nations, although both these nations are very flawed.

The ten horns that the woman has, as stated earlier, are the makeup of the beast's defenses, as the great ram uses to fight against the he-goat in Daniel chapter 8:3-12. But here, all the knowledge past and present will be used against the Lord God, "who is Lord of Lords, and King of Kings." God will overcome them and chain the beast for a thousand years, as will be shown in succeeding paragraphs. The angels go to explain in passage 15: "And he said to me, 'The waters that thou sawest where the harlots sits, are peoples and nations and tongues. And the ten horns that thou sawest, and the beast, theses will hate the harlot, and will make her desolate and naked, and will eat her flesh, and will burn her up in fire. For God has put it into their hearts to carry out His purpose, to give their kingdom to the beast, until the words of God are accomplished and the woman whom thou sawest is the great city which has kingship over the kings of the earth.'"

Here the people of earth along with the wayward kingdoms will realize their mistake and hate the woman, or the sins they caused, because she has caused them much anguish. But of course, God intended it to be that way, and His words, or will, always come to pass.

Chapter 18 tells about the fall of Babylon and how all laments her. "And after this I saw another angel coming down from heaven, having great authority, and the earth was lighted up by his glory. And he cried out with a mighty voice, saying she has fallen, she has fallen, Babylon the great; and has become a habitation of demons, a stronghold of every unclean spirit, a stronghold of every unclean and hateful bird; because all the nations have drunk of the wrath of her immorality, and the kings of the earth have committed fornication with her, and by the power of her wantonness the merchants of the earth have grown rich."

St. John goes on to tell of punishment that God will inflict on Babylon, and a voice from heaven tells the inhabitants, "Go out from her, my people, that you may not share in her sins, and that you may not receive of her plagues." The inhabitants are told to leave because Babylon's sins are great and have reached God. The voice tell how one day her plagues shall come, "death and mourning and famine; and she shall be burnt up in fire, for strong is God who will judge her." The verse goes on to say how the king's merchants and mariners will mourn over the death of Babylon; they all were with her and her ways.

At the end of the chapter, St. John tells how a strong angel took a stone and cast it into the sea saying, "With this violence will Babylon, the great city, be overthrown, and will not be found anymore. Nothing will stir within her gates, because for by thy sorcery all the nations have been led astray. And in her was found blood of prophets and of saints, and of all who have been slain upon the earth."

Chapter 19 is begun with an angelic song giving glory to God for His judgments are true and just. With the angelic song, the twenty-four elders, and the four living creatures fell down and worshiped God, who sits on the throne. After the angelic song comes the song of triumph. St. John hears the voice of many waters and the voice of mighty thunders saying, "Alleluia: for the Lord, out God almighty, now reigns: Let us be glad and rejoice, and give glory to Him: for the marriage of the Lamb has come, and His spouse has prepared herself." St. John also began to worship, and he is told to worship God for the testimony of Jesus is the spirit of prophecy.

CHAPTER 17

THE DIVINE WARRIOR

St. John sees Christ seated on a white horse. "And he who sat upon it is called Faithful and True, and with justice he judges and wages war. And his eyes are as a flame of fire, and on his head are many diadems, he has a name written no man knows except himself. And he is clothed in a garment sprinkled with blood, and his name is called the Word of God. And the armies of heaven, clothed in fine linen, white and pure, were following him on white horses."

In chapter 19, the beast and the false prophets are defeated. An angel calls with a loud voice all the birds in midheaven to come eat the flesh of those who are slain. The beast was seized, and with it the false prophet who did sorceries to deceive the people of earth to accept the mark of the beast. These two were cast alive into the pool of fire that burns with brimstone.

After the limited atomic war, which was fought in chapter 9, God began to prepare for the culmination of the earth. A sequence in chapters 11 and 12 tells of the entire struggle with Satan. At this point, the struggle is just about to be halted for a while.

Chapter 13 describes the story of how God lets seven great nations reign. Great in terms of earthly standards because all of these nations were blasphemous to God; the majority were pagan, as discussed earlier, with the rest enslaved to great sins.

Satan, in an attempt to win, in chapter 19, will take on God's chosen ones in a final great war. It is hard to determine here if there will be a war of a great magnitude than human beings can muster, or just satanic forces within man, Satan causing men to war against a holy nation. In any event, a halt to Satan's troubling mankind will be started after chapter 19. This can be seen by verse 20. "And the beast was seized, and with it the false prophets who did signs before it wherewith he deceived those who accepted the mark of he beast and who worshiped its image. These were cast into the pool of fire that burns with brimstone."

A key to the unraveling of this chapter is in the verse. "And the rest were killed with the sword of him who sits upon the horse, the sword that goes forth out of his mouth; and all the birds were filled with their flesh."

Of course, the foregoing passage refers to Christ, and it is His words, or preaching, that will dispel evil because he preaches the words of God the Father. These words will not be adhered to, and the souls of those who will not adhere to it will be lost forever.

Therefore, man has a key to the chapter since the word of Christ is always a sword and not meant in the physical sense. Perhaps the seizing of Satan and the false prophets were not done in the eyes of man. It seems as though after the destruction of a nation, which was physically destroyed, in chapter 18, God stopped everything at that point.

Satan and the false prophets were contained in the pool of fire, and every soul on earth was called upon to face the word of God. Those who were found faithful lived through the "standoff," and those who did not adhere to God's words and fell subject to Satan and the false prophets, died. Chapter 20 shows how God always gives man a second chance, or a chance to redeem himself.

Christ, promised from the beginning, had come and saved those who had kept the word of God after hearing them. He is truly the Divine Warrior because He warred with Satan and was victorious. Through His life, preaching, teachings, and death, Satan is defeated. As God, He suffered a great deal for man to be saved. But His glory is in the Father; therefore, He gladly gave

His all for God's creation, man, to be saved. Now it is almost complete; the long struggle is almost at its end with only the final test remaining, then eternal peace for those who believed and kept the word of God follows, and eternal damnation for those who preferred the beasts and the false prophets, or the world.

CHAPTER 18

THE FINAL TEST

In chapter 20, Satan is chained for a thousand years and is cast into the abyss, which is sealed "that he should deceive the nations no more, until the thousand years should be finished." God will test the faithful in His kingdom by unleashing Satan one more time after the thousand years are over. There are two resurrections: the martyrs will be the first, then the rest of the people who died. The martyrs will live with Christ the first thousands years and serve Him. This is the first resurrection; the second death has no power. They will not be judged again but will reign with God.

After the thousand years are finished, Satan will be released from his prison and will go forth and deceive the nations that are in the four corners of the earth—Gog and Magog—and will gather them together for the battle, the number of which is as the sand of the sea. "And they went up over the breath of the earth and encompassed the camp of the saints, and the beloved city. And fire from God came down out of heaven and devoured them. And the devil who deceived them was cast into the pool of fire and brimstone, where are also the beast and the false prophets; and they will be tormented day an night forever and ever."

Biblical time has always been of concern to many theologians, especially the days of Creation. The Bible says it took six days to create the earth, but science says it took millions of years for life to evolve to the present point. Do you take the Bible literally when it says six days, or does it mean that time in the term of days was given as a reference point?

The Bible is uniquely, extremely accurate because it is the word of God, and God's words are never in error. Therefore, evolution is an endowment by God to, let's say, keep the ball rolling or simply to create without His creating. This is why God in Genesis uses the term "seed after their own kind" (Gn 1:12, 21, 25, and 29).

The great zoologist Charles Darwin, in his theory of evolution, noticed this ability in creatures to adapt to changing environments many years ago. His discoveries are argued even now. He noticed that creatures actually change form as nature dictates their environments. Without this feature, many animals would not have survived and would have become extinct. Therefore, one can see many varied species of many things, plants and animals. Possibly, it took millions of years for them to evolve after God created the initial species

However, the argument goes on and on between theology and science, both claiming that they are correct and the other wrong. As Christians, we are to believe in the word of God that it took six days for Him to create the world and the things found on it. It is a part of our faith.

That is one time element that has been disputed for centuries. But using the basis of time in regard to Revelation, it can be shown that time in the Bible is the actual time that is meant, with possible exception to the difference in calendars.

If one were to look at the passage of the woman and the beast again—"And the woman fled into the wilderness, where she has a place prepared by God, that there may be nourished her a thousand two hundred and sixty days"—it is approximately three years and a month or two.

Since it was explained that the passage was referring to the Christ story, then one can go to the scriptures to verify that the time is real time. Going to the Gospel of St. Matthew, where the story of Christ is told, can do this.

In Matthew chapters 1 and 2, the whole story of Christ is told. The particular segment that explains the time mentioned is found in verse 13 of chapter 2, which reads: "Arise and take the child and his mother and flee into Egypt, and remain there until I tell thee." This was done by St. Joseph, and they remained there until the death of Herod. To prove that the time was actual time and that Christ actually was hidden in Egypt, the prophet's words regarding this were: "Out of Egypt I called my son" (Mt 2:15).

These words were written many years before the event took place and as it is with God, all prophecies come to pass or happen.

Therefore, this clearly shows that Christ was brought to Egypt to be safe and remained there until He was three years old, which is another symbol that is taking form, three being a number for the Trinity. The child was saved and returned to His countrymen, and the holy family settles in Galilee in a town called Nazareth, where another prophecy was fulfilled: "He shall be called the Nazarene."

There are far too many symbols using the numbers 3, 7, and 12 throughout the Bible to list as proof of the accuracy. Many are stated in this text and should be proof enough for the reader, and with that one can see that the foregoing is correct. Christ at the age of three, free from danger, fulfilled the first part of the prophecy, and with that the proof of time in the Bible being actual (a day as being a twenty-four-hour day) is verified.

Therefore, when the passage says that Satan will be chained for a thousand years, it means literally that he will be bounded for that many years, and at the end of those thousand years, he will be freed to deceive the nations once again.

To test the people of the earth as a final test of steadfastness to God, Satan will be released to deceive them again. But the martyrs who died will not be tested with the people or nations of earth, but will remain with Christ those thousand years to serve Him.

The martyrs are in the first resurrection and the second death has no power over them, the second death being the non-martyrs population, which will rest until it is time to release Satan once again for their final test.

God, throughout the existence of the world, has always given man a chance to redeem himself. Here, even at the end, man is given another chance to repent for his ways. However, it is his last chance. There can be no other. Either he will be counted among the faithful or perish with Satan and his followers, who already are doomed. Satan has nothing to lose because he has lost.

After the second defeat of the devil, the last judgment begins. St. John sees "the dead, the great and the small, standing before the throne, and scrolls were opened. And another was opened, which is the book of life; and the dead were judged out of those things that were written in the scrolls, according to their works. And the sea gave up the dead that were in it, and death and hell gave up the dead that were in them; and they were judged each one, according to their works. And hell and death were cast into the pool of fire. This is the second death, the pool of fire. And if anyone was not found written in the book of life, he was cast into the pool of fire."

Our life on earth is just a test to see if men are righteous enough for God to be with them, to walk with mankind. Adam was tested and failed his test; therefore, all mankind must be tested as Adam was. However, God, through His Divine wisdom, knew from the beginning that man would have to learn to be good. Since Adam chose knowledge, everything must be learned. This is the reason for the prophets' and Christ's mission, for man to learn the right way, how to be in accord with God. The prophets and Christ taught mankind kind about God the Father and His will for mankind.

Since our ways are not God's ways and our thoughts not His thoughts, God, because of His never-ending love for mankind, decided to allow man to be reconciled back to Him. The above is that plan. In simplicity, God will let everyone know that He is real, He actually exists as all the prophets and Christ has told. Then He will punish those who did not fare well the first time. This punishment will be so severe that all who go through will never forget it. At the same time all the sins they committed will stay right at hand while they are tormented for them. For instance, if you lied, you will hear all the lies you told over and over again until your time for punishment is up. This is true for all sin. It will be with you until your time is up. That is the first death.

After the first death, God will let man live for a thousand years; then He will lose Satan again to see if the lesson was learned. Those who do not stay good in the face of Satan this time will be lost forever in hell. However, the men who were God's saints will not be subject to the second test. They will pass with flying colors the first time, their character will never change; therefore, God will not subject them to any other suffering. They have shown God that they are truly and genuinely good.

If you could think of how much it hurts to be burnt, then you know that you would never allow yourself to be burnt again. In treating many illnesses such as certain addictions, the addict is subjected to sickness. He is made to be harshly sick by the substance that he abuses so that psychologically he will stop abusing the substance that he is hooked on. The pain will be remembered before the pleasure he derived from that substance; therefore, he is cured from abusing that substance.

This is the same method that God is using, but to a greater extent. The suffering in hell is so great that Christ explained that it is better to pluck your eye out, if it causes you to sin, rather then to face the fires of hell (Mt 5:29). With that great suffering, man is cleansed as gold and silver is cleansed by fire or fine braze is cleansed.

God went through great pains to bring all men to Himself. Each man has his own choice, either be with God in paradise or suffer in eternal hell. We all are eternal creatures, and we have to be contained by God. At the end, there are only two choices, paradise or hell. Christ said while He was on earth, "Take my yoke upon you and learn, for my yoke is easy and my burden light." Love is what God wants to see from all men. Love and righteousness is His order. This is easy to do since it is ingrained within every one of us to be such caring, loving, and obedient beings.

CHAPTER 19

THE NEW HEAVEN AND EARTH

Heaven and earth passed away with the coming of the last judgment; therefore, at the beginning of the chapter 21, a new heaven and new earth are formed. The new earth has no sea. St. John sees the New Jerusalem coming down from heaven from God. "And he heard a loud voice from the throne saying, 'Behold the dwelling of God with men, and he will dwell with them. And they will be his people, and God Himself will be with them as their God. And God will wipe away every tear from their eyes. And death shall be no more, neither shall there be mourning, nor crying, nor pain any more, for the former things have passed away.'"

God makes a promise that "to him that thirst, he will give of the fountain of the water of life freely. He who overcomes shall posses these things and I will be his God, and he shall be my son. But as for the cowardly and unbelieving, and abominable and murderers, and fornicators and sorcerers, and idolaters, and all liars, their portion shall be in the pool that burns with fire and brimstone, which is the second death."

After the promise that God kept, St. John was shown the New Jerusalem by the angel who had the bowl full of the seven last plagues. St. John was also made to measure the city, which had perfect measurements. The foundation of the wall of the city is like the stones used to name the tribes of Israel. The only difference is that the jasper stone is first and the sardius is sixth. This means that the new order of things is complete. Earth has been destroyed and now is perfect because Christ is ruling the earth. At first, the jasper stone was sixth, meaning green and imperfect, with the sardius first. The sardius stone is clear, blemish free, and perfect.

Chapter 22 gives a final description of the New Jerusalem, the river of the water of life, which means all life comes from God. This symbol is like the sea of glass meaning God gave life and He alone can take it. The river is coming forth from the throne of God and of the Lamb. Note that in the midst of the city street, on both sides of the river, was the tree of life, bearing twelve fruits, yielding its fruits according to each month. The leaves are for the healing of the nations. This is a reverse symbolism that God once ended paradise because Adam ate of the forbidden fruit. Now God placed in New Jerusalem a tree of eternal life.

St. John goes on to describe the throne of God and the Lamb: "And there shall be no more any accursed thing: but the throne of God and of the Lamb shall be in it, and His servants shall serve Him. And they shall see His face and His and His name shall be no more, and they shall have no need of light of lamp, or light of sun, for the Lord God will shed light upon them; and they shall reign forever and ever."

Chapter 22 concludes with St. John saying that everything will be the way he said it will happen and are true, that he was shown these things by an angel of the Lord.

These are Christ's words:

> Do not seal up the words of the prophecy of this book: for the time is at hand. He who does wrong, let him do wrong still; and he who is filthy, let him be filthy still; and he who is just, let him be just still; and he who is holy, let him be hollowed still. Behold, I come quickly! And my reward is with me, to render to each according to his works: I am the Alpha and the Omega, the first and the last, the beginning and the end. Blessed are they who wash their robes that they may have the right to the tree of life, and that by the gates they may enter into

the city. Outside are the dogs, and the sorcerers, and the fornicators, and the murderers, and the idolaters, and everyone who loves and practices falsehood.

Jesus's final attestation:

I Jesus have sent my angel to testify to you these things concerning the churches. I am the root and the offspring of David, the bright morning star. And the spirit and the bride say "come." And let him who hears say come: and let him who thirst come; and he who wishes, let him receive the water of life freely. I testify to everyone who hears the words of the prophecy of this book. If anyone shall add to them, God will add unto him the plagues that are written in this book. And if anyone shall take away from the word of the book this prophecy, God will take away his portion from the tree of life, and from the holy city, and from the things that are written in this book. He who testifies to these things say, "It is true, I come quickly!" Amen; Come Lord Jesus. The grace of our Lord Jesus Christ be with all, Amen.

Conclusion

Everyone should have a better understanding of the Bible, how it reads, it purpose, and should have come to the realization that God exists. There is no book that is so rich with guidance, so rich with beautiful flowing verses, so rich with stories of heroism and love, treachery and deceit, mystery and suspense. It is a treasure that will never be equaled, and the reader, after completion, should have a deeper faith in God since only such a being could effect this.

The proofs that are laid before you are simple proofs, even my authenticity, but this is how God operates. He uses simplicity to confound the so-called lofty of mind. The proof of the continent where Israel sits is a dramatic proof of the existence of God. Every time one looks at a map of the world and sees that shape of a foot with a prominent heel as if crushing down should be reminded of the promise that God made to Adam right after his fall, which was to send a redeemer for sins, Christ, into the world. God, by sending Christ in the flesh, is crushing the devil's head every time He wins a soul to God's side. Of course, the devil is still striking at that heel because he will never give up trying to gain souls, and the struggle goes on. The point is very graphic and pronounced and brings glory and honor to God because the promise is etched into the world for all mankind to see.

This etching was done millions of years before man was placed on earth and in itself proves the existence of God. It also proves that this book is authentic because the author lives in a state shaped in the form of a foot with a pronounced heel. This is no coincidence, but rather designed by God as a proof that the author is a ward of God as he claims to be and truly a prophet.

If one can truly understand the significance of the etching, then one can believe in all the clergy who are trying to lead him to God, thus save his eternal soul. It takes knowledge of God to be saved. If this knowledge is not imparted, then there is a greater chance that souls can and will be lost. God the Father stated this many times in the Old Testament. That knowledge is given in the Bible. It is a complete guide to heaven if it is adhered to rigidly. All obstacles are mapped out for the reader. If not understood through self-study, then there are hordes of clergy who strive each and every day and way to win souls for God. Many are very astute in the word of God and strict attention should be given to them. A large percentage of the television evangelists are excellent. Ninety—nine percent are not only diligent with their preaching and teaching but are very correct with the same. It can be seen that Christ really has His hands on them and guides them when they expound on the word.

This same word was promised by God to be preached throughout the world to all generations and peoples before the end (Is 66:19). When it is accomplished, the elect of God along with those who have heeded the word will be placed in a new paradise. For the former heaven and earth will pass way. God will make things new for mankind and as with the beginning it will be a joyous, beautiful, and perfect world—no more suffering or grief. "And I will rejoice in Jerusalem and joy in my people, and the voice of weeping shall no more be heard in her, nor the voice of crying" (Is 65:18).

This book, as stated, is meant to wake a sleeping world up to God's time frame and it is not meant to alarm but to enlighten and broaden one's knowledge of God and His will for mankind. A profound groundwork has been done by many countless men of God to prepare the world for the Second Coming of Christ, which is the judgment of the world. Everyone that lived on this earth from great to small will be judged by Christ to give an account of His life here on this earth.

Many things were given a brief so that the book would not be cluttered, but those things needed to be presented so that the reader could get a better picture of the Divine and the purposeful order of the world, or God's intent for all existence. There will be other books addressing those things in detail, such as the Trinity, the metaphysical or supernatural, and others addressed in this book, which are difficult to understand.

God went through great pains to continue man's life. All was almost lost if not for the heart of one man, Noah, a righteous soul. Through Noah's seed, a second chance was allowed for man to live and experience that life in a beautiful sensuous setting, which is a precious gift. This is especially so at the end of the existing world where everything will be perfect once again. That will be a very glorious day!